Programming Language: 3 Books in 1

Beginner's Guide to Programming Code with Python

Best Practices to Programming Code with Python

Advanced Guide to Programming Code with Python

Charlie Masterson

© Copyright 2017 by Charlie Masterson - All rights reserved.

The following Book is reproduced below with the goal of providing information that is as accurate and reliable as possible. Regardless, purchasing this Book can be seen as consent to the fact that both the publisher and the author of this book are in no way experts on the topics discussed within and that any recommendations or suggestions that are made herein are for entertainment purposes only. Professionals should be consulted as needed prior to undertaking any of the action endorsed herein.

This declaration is deemed fair and valid by both the American Bar Association and the Committee of Publishers Association and is legally binding throughout the United States.

Furthermore, the transmission, duplication or reproduction of any of the following work including specific information will be considered an illegal act irrespective of if it is done electronically or in print. This extends to creating a secondary or tertiary copy of the work or a recorded copy and is only allowed with express written consent from the Publisher. All additional right reserved.

The information in the following pages is broadly considered to be a truthful and accurate account of facts and as such any inattention, use or misuse of the information in question by the reader will render any resulting actions solely under their purview. There are no scenarios in which the publisher or the original author of this work can be in any fashion deemed liable for any hardship or damages that may befall them after undertaking information described herein.

Additionally, the information in the following pages is intended only for informational purposes and should thus be thought of as universal. As befitting its nature, it is presented without assurance regarding its prolonged validity or interim quality. Trademarks that are mentioned are done without written consent and can in no way be considered an endorsement from the trademark holder.

Table of Contents

Beginner's Guide to Programming Code with Python

Introduction
Chapter 1: Hatching Your Python
Chapter 2: Python Variables, Math, and Comments
Chapter 3: Conditionals and Booleans
Chapter 4: Lists and Loops
Chapter 5: Functions
Chapter 6: File I/O
Chapter 7: String Manipulation
Chapter 8: Basic Object-Oriented Programming: Objects and Classes
Chapter 9: More on Object-Oriented Programming and Classes
Chapter 10: Book List Redux
Conclusion

Best Practices to Programming Code with Python

Introduction
Chapter 1: General Concepts of Python Coding
Chapter 2: Programming Recommendations
Chapter 3: Code Layout
Chapter 4: Idioms
Chapter 5: Comments
Chapter 6: Conventions
Chapter 7: Method and Function Arguments
Chapter 8: Naming Conventions
Chapter 9: Using Whitespace in Statements and Expressions
Conclusion

Advanced Guide to Programming Code with Python

Introduction
Chapter 1: Python Comprehensions
Chapter 2: Python Iterators
Chapter 3: Python Generators
Chapter 4: Python Decorators
Chapter 5: Python Context Managers
Chapter 6: Python Descriptors Overview
Chapter 7: Using Python Descriptors
Chapter 8: Metaprogramming
Chapter 9: An Overview of Python Scripting Blender
Bonus Chapter: Django Web Development with Python
Conclusion
About the Author

About this Bundle:

Congratulations on owning *Programming Language: 3 Books in 1 - Beginner's Guide, Best Practices and Advanced Guide to Programming Code with Python* and thanks for doing so.

What you are about to read is a collection of three separate books on how to learn Python computer programming.

Each book will discuss different levels towards learning Python, arranged in proper order that takes you from **beginner** to **intermediate** and **advanced** level.

Book 1:
<u>Python: Beginner's Guide to Programming Code with Python</u>

Here you will learn the basic essentials of learning Python – the necessary topics you require in gaining beginner level knowledge.

Book 2:
<u>Python: Best Practices to Programming Code with Python</u>

Here you will progress and learn intermediate

level Best Practices to help you write more efficient Python code.

Book 3:
Python: Advanced Guide to Programming Code with Python

Here you will progress even further and learn Advanced Python programming and learn advanced Python topics – to help you progress in your path towards Python mastery.

Thanks again for owning this book!

Let us begin with the first book in the Python bundle:

Python:

Beginner's Guide to Programming Code with Python

Charlie Masterson

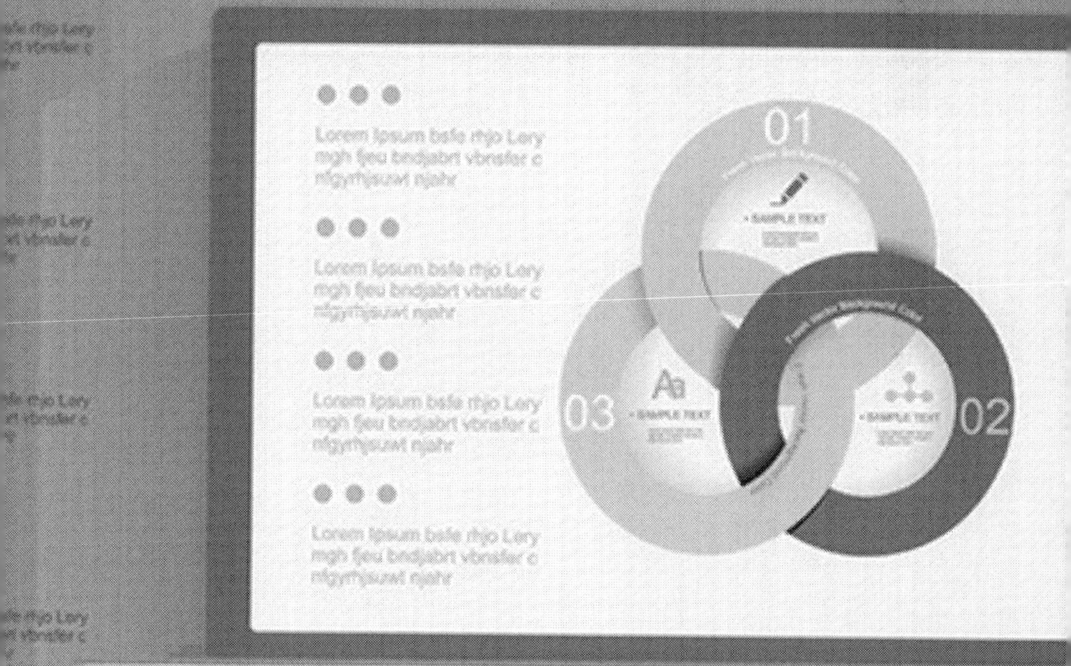
Lorem ipsum bsfe rhjo Lery
mgh fjeu bndjabrt vbnsfer c
nfgyrhjsuwl njahr
Lorem ipsum bsfe rhjo Lery
mgh fjeu bndjabrt vbnsfer c
nfgyrhjsuwl njahr
Lorem ipsum bsfe rhjo Lery
mgh fjeu bndjabrt vbnsfer c
nfgyrhjsuwl njahr
Lorem ipsum bsfe rhjo Lery
mgh fjeu bndjabrt vbnsfer c
nfgyrhjsuwl njahr
01
SAMPLE TEXT
02
SAMPLE TEXT
03
Aa
SAMPLE TEXT

Introduction

Congratulations on owning *Python: Beginner's Guide to Programming Code with Python* and thanks for doing so.

The following chapters will discuss the Python programming language, how to get started, and how to program in Python - starting at the most simple concepts and helping you to create real world applications by the end of the book.

I say it a lot near the end, but it's only because it's true: programming is the apex of self-expression for a great number of people. There are a great many things you can accomplish using Python, and an even greater number of things if you're looking at the big picture of the all-encompassing everything of computers and programming.

We're going to help you get set and get on the path to being the best programmer that you can possibly be. Even if you're an absolute and total novice, you'll find this book easy to comprehend and work through, as well as engaging enough to not be an absolute and total bore as some programming books can very much be.

All in all, there are many things to be said about Python, and we may just scratch the surface - but that surface will be enough to prepare you for any and everything you will encounter going forward in the language.

That is to say, there are plenty of books on this subject on the market, thanks again for choosing this one! Every effort was made to ensure it is full of as much useful information as possible, please enjoy!

Chapter 1: Hatching Your Python

Python is one of the most popular programming languages out there today, full stop. There are few languages as prolific as Python has become. Python is a beautiful and multi-purpose language which can be found everywhere from on web servers to running video games to being the powerhouse behind popular applications.

Learning Python is a huge boon to you as a person in several ways. The largest is, of course, you're learning a programming language. Learning a programming language in general opens up a huge number of possibilities for the things which you can do with a computer. It can be a career skill and a hobby, too.

Python in particular is a fantastic language to learn because it can be used for a multitude of things. It's simple enough for beginners to grasp easily and, though simple, it's incredibly powerful.

In order to use Python, you need to set it up. You can set up Python on Windows, Mac, and Linux. For the purposes of this book, I personally will be using a Linux system, but the instructions should be relatively straightforward and apply to every operating system.

In order to set up Python, you first need to grab a text editor. Many will work and many are out there indeed: I personally will be using Atom, which you can download from the website atom.io. Notepad++ and Sublime Text are also fantastic options.

After you've got your text editor, you need to check to be sure you have Python installed. Go to your Terminal (or Powershell in Windows) and try to run the command *python*. If Python isn't installed (it says something along the lines of *command "python" not recognized*), then you need to install it.

In order to install it, you need to go to Python.org and grab Python 2.7.12 for your respective platform.

After it's installed, make sure it's working again - it should be.

You're going to be using your Terminal/PowerShell to navigate and execute files, so you need to know how to navigate using those. If you don't know, I highly suggest doing a Google search on the topic. There are a ton of very simple tutorials on the subject, but for brevity's sake, I'd like to avoid going to in-depth on extraneous things as such.

Now we're going to work on writing and running your first program.

Go into your text editor and create a new file. Save it before you even start writing code, because then you'll have access to syntax highlighting which will help you out a fair amount. You can save it under whatever name you'd like going forward, but for the purpose of this example, you need to save it as *first.py*.

In the text file, type the following:

```
print "hello world"
```

Then head back to your Terminal or PowerShell and navigate to where you saved the file.

Run it by the following command:

```
python first.py
```

What happens? It should run perfectly and print out "hello world" to the console.

Now let's go back and change that text file a bit more. Let's add a few lines.

```
print "hello world"
print "my name is [type your name here]"
print "it's nice to meet you"
```

Save the file and execute it again. It should print across multiple lines.

Awesome! We're done with your very first program. We're going to be messing with this file a little in the coming chapters in order to teach you important fundamentals of Python.

Chapter 2: Python Variables, Math, and Comments

When you were younger, you probably took a basic algebra class where you'd have to work with equations like $y = mx + b$. You could actually fill in these letters with other values in order to give you y. These values were called variables.

Variables in programming are somewhat similar. Variables are ways to give a name to a value so that you can use it throughout your program. Variables aren't restricted to numbers, though.

Go back to your *first.py* file and a few lines above your print statements, type the following, with your name in the quotations:

```
name = "John Doe"
```

Afterwards, go back to the line which says "My name is [your name]" and rewrite it to be the following:

```
print "my name is " + name
```

Then save and run it in console. It should say "my name is " along with whatever you wrote in the quotations. Go ahead and modify the string some more, add a y, do whatever you want to do to it really, then save and execute it again.

The way that variables work is that they store a value to a name. Python makes working with variables very, very easy compared to other languages. Since it's a scripting language, it's rather straightforward with the way that it allows you to type variables. Scripting languages are intended to have you up-and-running as soon as possible and waste as little time as possible, staying out of your way while you create your program.

    The variable we just created is called a "string", which is a set of characters. Every time you print something to the console, you're printing out a string. If you're only printing out string values, you can use the + in order to concatenate the strings, which is a fancy word meaning put them together. In order to properly include other kinds of variables in your code, however, you need to use a formatted string.

```
print "my name is %s" % name
```

    There are a number of formatted types you can use, but for right now, just remember that:

    %s -   prints a string
    %d -   prints a base-10 number
    %f -   prints a float
    %r -   prints the raw data of the variable (used for debugging)

    As I just implied, there are more kinds of variables beyond strings that you can use. Let's do some work with numbers. Create a new script. I'm going to call mine *fruit.py*. In Atom, you do this by right-clicking the sidebar where your files are listed and clicking "New file". When it prompts you for the path, you can simply type the file name.

Firstly, there's a type of variable called an integer in other languages which is essentially a whole number. Let's say that you had four apples and your friend had six apples, and you wanted to see how many apples you had altogether. You could type something along the lines of:

```
myApples = 4
friendApples = 6
totalApples = myApples + friendApples
```

The variable *myApples* would have the value of 4, while the variable *friendApples* would have the value of 6, and *totalApples* would take the value of the variable *myApples* added to *friendApples*.

You can check all of these values by typing some print commands below that.

```
print "I have %d apples." % myApples
print "My friend has %d apples." % friendApples
print "Together, we have %d apples." % totalApples
```

Save and run. It should print out something along the lines of the following:

```
I have 4 apples.
My friend has 6 apples.
Together, we have 10 apples.
```

Let's say you gained one more apple, maybe picked it off a tree or something, and now you have 5 apples. Can you think of how you would write this?

Type the following below your print statements.

```
print "I got one more apple!"

myApples = myApples + 1

print "I now have %d apples." % myApples
print "Now we have %d apples altogether!" % totalApples
```

Save and run that file. You'll notice there's an error - you should have *eleven* apples altogether, but it says you've only got 10. This is because you'd set the value of totalApples earlier when myApples was only 4, and you need to set it again.

Below your myApples = myApples + 1 statement, add:

```
totalApples = myApples + friendApples
```

That should fix any problems that you've got with your totalApples variable.

I should also make the distinction, since we're formatting strings right now, that if you need to format a number of variables within a string, they need to go within parentheses. For example, if we wanted to combine line one and two into "I have *x* apples and my friend has *y* apples", we would write the following in our code:

```
"I have %d apples and my friend has %d apples." % (myApples, friendApples)
```

Additionally, while we're dealing with numbers, we should probably talk about Python math. Python handles math expressions by way of something called operators.

The general operators are self-explanatory:

+	-	addition
-	-	subtraction
*	-	multiplication
/	-	division
%	-	modulus (finds remainder)
**	-	exponentiation (2**4 is 2 to the power of 4)
//	-	floor division

Then there are assignment operators. To add 1 to myApples earlier, we typed "*myApples = myApples + 1*". You can shorten this, though, to *myApples += 1*.

Assignment operators are as follows:

=	-	x = y
+= y	-	x = x + y
-= y	-	x = x - y
*= y	-	x = x * y
/= y	-	x = x / y
%= y	-	x = x % y

$**= y$ - $\quad x = x ** y$
$//= y$ - $\quad x = x // y$

You can use these to assign values to a given numeric variable and perform assignment operations.

In addition to those operators and variables, there's also another type of variable called a boolean, which evaluates the truth of a statement.

These are statements are evaluated with comparison operators, which are as such:

$x == y$ - x is equal to y
$x != y$ - x is not equal to y
$x > y$ - x is greater than y
$x < y$ - x is less than y
$x >= y$ - x is greater than or equal to y
$x <= y$ - x is less than or equal to y

Let's say that you and your friend got in an argument over who has more apples, and you were spitefully complaining to your text editor because you're certain that you have more apples.

Create a new variable below your current chunk of code called "moreApples".

Let's set this to the truth of the expression "myApples is greater than friendApples", like so:

```
moreApples = myApples > friendApples
```

Then below that, type the following:

```
print "My friend says he has more apples! That's not even %r!" % moreApples
```

Save the file and run from your terminal. The output should look like the following:

```
$ python fruit.py
I have   4   apples.
My friend has   6   apples.
Together, we have   10   apples.
I gained one more apple!
I now have   5   apples!
Now we have   11   apples altogether!
My friend says he has more apples.
That's not even   False !
```

Ah... well, this is slightly embarrassing. But it's right, it's not false when your friend says he has more apples - perhaps you should relearn basic arithmetic before you get into arguments with your friends regarding the amounts of things.

So because the statement *myApples > friendApples* is false and your amount of apples isn't actually greater than your friend's apples, the variable *moreApples* stored the value False. If it were *myApples < friendApples*, then it would have stored the value True.

There's one more type of variable called floating-point, which is essentially decimal numbers. This doesn't fit terribly well into the idea of apples, but you'd declare a float variable like this:

```
percentageOfMyFriendThatRolfIsFollowingOurArgumentAboutApples = 0.3
```

You may be asking why Rolf is still .3 my friend after an argument about apples. Allow me to explain in code:

```
percentageOfMyFriendThatRolfIsFollowingOurArgumentAboutApples = 0.3
    # Rolf is still 30% my friend because he let me borrow his truck to move.
```

Whoa! What's this? Well, the technical name is an octothorpe, but it's also called a "hash" and the "pound sign". But it's used to lead off comments in your code. Comments are parts of your code that the compiler ignores when it's preparing your code to be read for the computer.

You can place these over and over and the compiler will ignore them - fantastic for mid-code poetry breaks.

```
print "Oh, what a beautiful morning!"
    # Howl, by Allen Ginsberg
    # I saw the best minds of my generation destroyed by madness,
    #    starving, hysterical, naked,
    print "What a time to be alive!"
```

The compiler will only see the two print statements and ignore the society-questioning vitriol of 1950s Beat poetry. (Don't actually take mid-code poetry breaks, it's frowned upon.)

You can also use these after a line of code, and the compiler will ignore the rest of the line.

```
print "Rolf is my friend!" # just kidding
```

Comments, used sparingly, are a tool for absolute good and can help strangers (including yourself in the future when you stumble upon old code) to understand what you're trying to get at with any given chunk of code.

Avoid, however, using them too often. Overuse of comments makes code nauseating to read, and code should generally be self-explanatory anyway.

One last thing while we're working with print statements. We aren't going to use it too much right now, but it will come up later, and it's worth knowing: escape sequences. These are things you can use in Python in order to modify your text.

The first and foremost example is the newline escape sequence - "\n". This is used to designate that a string has a line break. Try printing the following:

```
print "Hello\nworld\nHow are you?"
```

Save and run this program. It should print across multiple lines.

Another thing you can use is the \t escape sequence, which places a tab between two characters, or at the beginning of a line:

```
print "I have:\n\t%d boxes of strawberries,\n\t%d apples, \n\t and %d peaches." % (2, 3, 4)
```

There are a few other escape characters. For example, if you need to write a single-quote or double-quote within a string, you have two options:

Encase the whole thing in triple quotes, like so:

```
"""He said "see you tomorrow," and that's all."""
```

Or escape them, like so:

```
"He said \"see you tomorrow,\" and that's all."
```

The same goes for backslashes - you have to escape them. These are the primary ones you'll be using, but a simple Google search will turn up the rest. They're generally very niche and are only useful for certain situations specific to program debugging or something along those lines. As a novice programmer just trying to find your way around the language, you won't find much use for them. That said, I won't stifle you, and if you're a creative or experimental person, you can probably get some fun results and outputs out of playing around with the other escape characters. By all means, do it.

To recap this chapter, we covered the essentials of variables and math. Those are massive pinnacles of programming, and it's imperative that you understand them as much as possible if you're really intending to go forward with programming because they make up the bulk of every major action your program will perform in one way or another. But with all of that done, it's now time to jump into the wide, wide world of conditionals and loops, where you will start to be exposed to Python's despotic indentation rules that are actually rather quaint.

Chapter 3: Conditionals and Booleans

Earlier on, we talked about comparison operators and how they could be used to determine whether a statement within a language was true or false. This is where we get into one of the biggest concepts underlying any given program. If things were such that you always knew one thing or another, the world would be a very different place. However, this really isn't the case, and there are times where you have to evaluate a situation, make a determination, and then make a decision regarding that condition.

These kinds of situations are often very serious and demand your utmost response. For example, if your friend Rolf, who doesn't understand basic apple arithmetic, were trying to log into your computer, you would want it to tell him to go away. So how would we go about this? (We're going to use our first command to accept user input in this script, so saddle in for that as well.)

Create a new script. Call it what you like - I'll be calling mine login.py.

We want to create a few variables called username and password. Set username and password to anything that you want.

Ask the user to enter their username, like so:

```
userInput = raw_input("What is your username? ")
```

Now we're going to work some magic and have Python decide whether they entered the described username or not.

```
if userInput == username:
    userInput = raw_input("Password? ")
else:
    print "You entered the incorrect username."
```

We're going to get to the else part in a second, but for now, just save this and try to run it. Test it by entering the wrong username first, then run the program again and enter the correct username. If all goes well, you'll see the proper responses.

Now let's talk about what's happening here.

This is called an if/else statement, and is the most basic form of conditional decision making within Python (and most programming languages, for that matter.)

What happens is that you give it a statement that it evaluates the truthfulness of a given statement and then takes action based off of whether or not the statement was true.

What is occurring in that chunk of code up there is that it's evaluating whether or not userInput -- which is the string that we just had the user enter -- is the same as "username". If it is, then it prompts the user for their password. If it isn't, then it tells them that they entered the wrong username. Simple enough, right?

But we do have that personal vendetta against Mr. Rolf, so we should probably include that within our code. But how? I mean, we've already got a completed if statement, right?

Wrong! There's another thing we can do, called an else if. Check this out:

```
if userInput == username:
        userInput = raw_input("Password? ")
    elif userInput == "rolf" or userInput == "Rolf" or userInput == "ROLF":
            print "There is no room on this computer for Rolf."
    else:
            print "You have entered the incorrect username."
```

This evaluates the userInput to see if the username is "Rolf" or any variant thereof. String comparison is innately case-sensitive, so "ROlf" would not be equal to "ROLf". How can we fix this?

Well, we can simultaneously fix the case-sensitivity issue and make the code more elegant by changing our else-if line to the following.

```
elif userInput.lower() == "rolf":
```

This converts whatever the userInput variable is to lower-case. We can now simply compare it to lower-case "rolf" and the issue would be fixed.

You may have noticed the little *"or"*, and it might have caught you off guard. That's called a boolean operator.

There are three primary boolean operators in Python: and, or, and not.

"And" is used to check two conditions and see if they both return true. If either returns false, then the whole thing returns false. So to use the apple values from the last script, if we were to write this:

```
if myApples == 5 and friendApples == 6:
```

It'd come back as true. However, if even *one* of those weren't true, the whole thing would return false.

"Or" is similar, but it checks to see if *either* condition or expression is true. If even one is true, the whole thing comes back true.

"Not" checks to see if a boolean/condition/expression is *not* true. For the sake of illustration and exposition, you can actually put a single boolean variable into an if-statement, because an if statement only checks to see if whatever following it is true.

If you had a variable called "IAmCool" which is set to True, and you typed:

```
if IAmCool:
    print "I am cool"
```

It would actually print "I am cool", because the if-statement sees that as a true statement. Following?

Now, if IAmCool were set to False because the only thing stronger than your self-deprecating sense of humor is your will to teach yourself various programming languages, and you instead of "if IAmCool" typed this:

```
if not IAmCool:
    print "I am not cool"
```

It would check to see if IAmCool were *false*.

So between if, else if, and else statements, you've got a pretty solid chunk of conditional decision making under wraps.

Let's go back to that code we had just a moment ago.

```
if userInput == username:
    userInput = raw_input("Password? ")
elif userInput.lower() == "rolf":
    print "There is no room on this computer for Rolf."
else:
    print "You have entered the incorrect username."
```

We got the username, and it was right. Where do we go from here?

This is where we start to utilize a concept known as *nested conditional statements*. You can put an if-statement within an if-statement!

This is your time to shine, friend. After prompting for the password, write another if-statement *within* that if-statement, as well as an else statement. You need to compare userInput to your variable password and see if they're the same. If they are, you need to welcome the user; if they aren't, you need to tell them that they've entered the wrong password.

By the end, your code should look like this:

```
if userInput == username:
    userInput = raw_input("Password? ")
    if userInput == password:
        print "Welcome!"
    else:
        print "That's the wrong password."
elif [...]
```

If it does, then you succeeded.

Chapter 4:
Lists and Loops

It's a little uncommon to put these two concepts in the same chapter, but I'm trying to be brief and they really do go hand in hand.

We've talked about variables, sure. But variables can only hold a single value. What if you had multiple values that you wanted to put in something? This is where lists come in handy.

Lists in Python are very straightforward.

Let's say that we wanted to create a list of our favorite TV shows. We could do this like so:

```
favoriteShows = ['Breaking Bad', 'Narcos', 'House of Cards']
```

These are all different elements in a list which starts counting at 0. You can also access the lists rather simply.

If you were to type the following:

```
print favoriteShows[0]
```

Then it would print out the first element of the list, here being Breaking Bad.

You can also enter data into a list rather simply! Lists have a built in function called "append()" which allows you to add data to the list, like so:

```
listExample.append(raw_input())
```

This would take the user's input and add it to the function. (It's also an example of calling a function as an argument of a function, which makes no sense at all right now but hopefully will in the next chapter!)

You can actually declare empty lists to be used, as well. You'd do so by declaring the variable and setting it with empty brackets, like this:

```
emptyList = []
```

From here, you could add elements to the list and start to use it like you would any other list.

To move to the next portion of the lesson and get off the whole list tangent, we should talk about loops. Loops are an integral part of many programs. They serve a great many purposes, but at their most basic level they're simply a way for a chunk of code within a program to repeat multiple times, most likely changing in one way or another each time.

There are three main kinds of loops in Python: while, for, and do...while. All of these have their own particular uses that they're tailored for.

While loops are the most simple, they execute over and over for as long as a given condition still comes back as true, and that's all there really is to it.

Observe the following code:

```
dogs = 0
while (dogs <= 10):
        print "There are %d dogs in the yard!"
        dogs += 1

print "Wow! That's a lot of dogs!"
```

Can you guess what's happening here? We declared a variable called dogs and we set it to 0. We then started the while loop, giving it a condition. *While* the variable dogs is less than or equal to 10, we want to run this loop. Every iteration of this loop will print "There are *x* dogs in the yard!", and the loop increments every single time.

For loops are similar to while loops, but they automatically increment over a set of data, such as the lists we were talking about earlier.

You don't necessarily have to iterate over lists. Python has a built-in range function that lets you iterate through a certain number of variables. For example, a for loop iterating through range(5) would iterate 5 times, from 0 to 4. Let's use this to count to 5.

Here's an example of that for loop:

```
for i in range(5):
        print "%d" % (i + 1)
```

Simple enough, right? Not too hard at all. We can also iterate through lists like earlier. If we wanted to print out every TV show on our list from earlier, we could do something like:

```
print "My favorite shows are: "
for i in favoriteShows:
    print "%s" % i
```

The *i* is what's called a loop variable, and in Python, it assumes the type of whatever your list is made of. Since lists can hold mixed values (even at once), this is great and super important.

Let's actually start working with this and combining a lot of the concepts that we've worked on.

Create a new file, call it what you like but I'm going to call mine bookList.py.

The first thing that we're going to do is create an empty list of books and a boolean called running set to True.

```
bookList = []
running = True
```

Now what we're going to do is create something called a running loop. This is to show you a way that while loops can be used.

We're going to create a loop that runs for as long as the variable "running" is true.

```
while running == True:
```

The first thing we're going to do within the loop is prompt the user to add a book, list the current books, or exit the program. We're going to want to compare the response to other things, so we need to set it to a variable.

```
            userInput = raw_input("Book List
v1.\nType \"add\" to add a book, \"list\"
to list the books, or \"exit\" to exit
the program: ")
```

Now we need to parse the input and compare it. First, we're going to see if the user wanted to add a book, and add a book if they did:

```
            if userInput.lower() == "add":
                userInput = raw_input("Enter
the name of the book: \n")
                bookList.append(userInput)
```

Perfect. There's actually a way to simplify that line by just passing the function "raw_input('…')" to bookList.append, but I wanted to show you that you can append any variable to your list.

Now we're going to determine what happens if the user entered "list", which should be checking to see if the list is empty and printing out its contents if not:

```
            elif userInput.lower() == "list":
                if not bookList: # this is
shorthand for "if the bookList is empty"
                    print "The list is
empty!\n"
                else:
                    for i in bookList:
                        print "%s\n" % i
# prints everything on the list
```

Now, if the user entered "exit", we need to set the variable running to false so that we exit the main loop, since it's only supposed to run while the variable running is true.

```
elif userInput.lower() == "exit":
    running = False
```

And lastly, if they entered anything *but* "add", "list", or "exit", we need to print that their command was invalid.

```
else:
    print "The command was invalid!\n"
```

This is the first major program we've done so far, but this is a very cursory introduction to variables, loops, and input/output.

From here on out, we're going to be introducing concepts by working on this specific file, so you need to hold this file near and dear.

Chapter 5: Functions

Functions are an integral part of any given programming language. They supply a way to define something that's supposed to happen and may have to happen many times or basic functions of the program in general, and reuse that chunk of code as often as you need to. They also allow you to modify existing values and work with variables that you already have.

The basic breakdown of a function in pseudocode is like this:

```
function(parameter1, parameter2, etc...) {
     do things
}
```

And it will normally be called within your main portion of code or from other functions like so:

function(*variable1, variable2*)

Functions can be used to massively simplify abrasively verbose code and make it much easier to understand, while at the same time making it more modular and reusable.

So how do you work with functions in Python? They follow a very simple structure.

In order to declare a function in Python, you simply type:

```
def functionName(arguments):
     code here
```

That's really all that there is to it. The parameters that you define for a function can be used within the body of that function's code. When you call the function later on, you can put any values of the same type in the place. The best way to explain it is that the parameters you use in your function definition are *hypothetical*, and are intended to be replaced with actual values.

If we wanted to code a function which was to take the length and width of a rectangle, find the area, and return that value, we could do it like this:

```
def findArea(length, width):
    return length * width
```

You could then call this later in your code. You can use actual values, like so:

```
area = findArea(4, 6) # "area" would have the value of 24
```

Or you can use already existent variables in order to call the function.

```
l = 6
w = 3
area = findArea(l, w) # "area" would have the value of 18
```

You can even use other functions as arguments, since every function simply returns a value.

```
def add(number1, number2):
    return number1 + number2
```

```
def findArea(length, width):
    return length * width

area = findArea(4, add(2,2))
```

This code would first do the add function which would return the value 4, then multiply the return value of the add function by the first argument (4). It would ultimately return the value of 16.

So the question now is, how can we use functions in order to pretty up our existing code and make it more functional? Let's go back to our bookList code. It's perfectly functional, right? But looking at it is a mess. Let's give functions to our addBook and listBook functions, and make them a little bit more, well, functional while we're at it.

So let's look at the if statement for adding a book.

```
if userInput.lower() == "add":
    userInput = raw_input("Enter the name of the book.\n"
    bookList.append(userInput)
```

What we want to do is make this so it's simpler, like so:

```
if userInput.lower90 == "add":
    addBook(bookList)
```

Here's how we'd do this. Functions have to be declared and defined before you call them. You can do it anywhere before. I'm going to do it at the beginning right after our variableList.

```
def addBook(bList):
    userInput = raw_input("Enter the name of the book you'd like to add.\n")
    bList.append(userInput)
```

You could have named the variable *bList* anything, even *bookList* - the reason I didn't name it bookList for simplicity's sake is in order to drive home the point that function parameters are only hypothetical values that you replace with real values when you call them.

Now if we replace our current if-statement with this:

```
if userInput.lower() == "add":
    addBook(bookList)
```

It should work perfectly fine.

Now we need to add a function which will allow us to list the books. This is going to be much the same: we need to send it our list, bookList, and have it read it off. First we need to define it. I'm putting it right after our last function:

```
def listBooks(listOfBooks):
```

Now we need to transfer our logic over.

```
def listBooks(listOfBooks):
    if not listOfBooks:
```

```
                    print "The list is
empty!\n"
        else:
            for i in listOfBooks:
                print "%s\n" % i
```

After that, we can go back to our if-statement and replace the ugly code with the far more elegant:

```
elif userInput.lower() == "list":
    listBooks(bookList)
```

Save and run your code to ensure that it works. It should go just fine. By the end, it should look a bit like this:

```
bookList = []
running = True

def addBook(bList):
    userInput = raw_input("Enter the name of the book you'd like to add.\n")
    bList.append(userInput)

def listBooks(listOfBooks):
    if not listOfBooks:
        print "The list is empty!\n"
    else:
        for i in listOfBooks:
            print "%s\n" % i

while running == True:
    userInput = raw_input("Book List v1.\nType \"add\" to add a book, \"list\" to list the books, or \"exit\" to exit\n")
    if userInput.lower() == "add":
        addBook(bookList)
```

```
        elif userInput.lower() ==
"list":
            listBooks(bookList)
        elif userInput.lower() ==
"exit":
            running = False
        else:
            print "The command was
invalid!\n"
```

Notice how much cleaner and easier to read that our primary code is, starting at the run loop and going to the end of the program.

Chapter 6:
File I/O

Alright, let's put the bookList away for a second, we'll come back to it momentarily after talking about file input/output and string manipulation, once we finally get to the chapter on object-oriented programming. For now, it's time to talk about reading and writing files.

There'll be many times in your programming career (or hobby) that you'll need to read or write data to a file. There are a crazy amount of applications for this, as well. If you were designing a game, you could save your player's progress. We could use it in our book list in order to export a list of books (intense foreshadowing.) Even the word processor I'm writing this on needs to export and import data from files constantly.

So how exactly do we do this in Python?

Python, like many other things, makes reading from and writing to a file relatively painless.

First what you'd have to do is open the file and give the value of said file to a variable, like so:

```
file1 = open('example', mode)
```

Mode can be many things. *w* for writing to a file only, *a* for appending to existing files, *r+* for reading and writing, and *r* to only be read. The *mode* part may be omitted, and if it is, then it will be assumed you are only reading the file.

Once the file is open, there are a few methods that you can use.

file1.*read(size)*, where size is optional. If size is included, it will read *size* amount of data and return it as a string, which you could assign to a variable or print or whatever, really. If you exclude *size*, it will read over the entire file and return the entire thing.

file1.*readline()* reads only a single line from a file, which can be very useful for certain applications where you need to feed data into a list or something along those lines.

file1.*write(string)* will write the contents of the given string to the file. If you want to write something that isn't a string, you'll need to actually cast it to a string.

```
liters = 2
str(liters)
file1.write(liters + "\n")
```

Or you'd have to do a format string, as such:

```
file1.write("There are %d liters" % liters)
```

Both are perfectly viable ways of achieving the end goal here.

When you're finished with a file, you always have to close it in order to free up system resources.

```
file1.close()
```

We're going to work with this a bit more in-depth in chapter 10 when we finally finish working with string manipulation and object-oriented concepts and start to synthesize a lot of what we learned, but for now, feel free to experiment with these concepts and try to make something happen using them.

Chapter 7: String Manipulation

There will almost certainly be times where you need to manipulate this string or that. Maybe you'll need to get its length, or you'll need to split it or make another string from it. Maybe you'll need to read what character is at *x* position. Whatever the reason is, the point is that there's a reason.

The reason that we're getting into this so late into the book is that it opens us up to a broader discussion on the nature of objects that we're going to go more in-depth within the next chapter, but in the meantime, we're also going to be covering extremely useful methods that the Python language provides to be used with strings.

Go ahead and create a new file. As always, you can call it whatever you want. My file is going to be named strings.py. Uncreative name, sure, but we're going to be getting creative with strings in this chapter, believe me.

So what is a string, really? Well, we obviously know that a string is a line of text, which goes without saying. But what goes into that?

We've spoken quite a bit in this list about *lists*. Lists are actually a form of another variable that's largely eschewed in Python programming called an *array*. An array is a pre-allocated set of data that goes together, in the most basic terms of speaking.

Python comes from and is built upon a language called C. In C, there are actually data types. There are data types in Python, too, but Python saves the user time by setting the data type *for* the programmer instead of having the programmer declare it.

One of the data types in C was called a *char*, which was a single character. In terms of computer speak; there isn't a native support for strings. Strings were simply arrays of characters. For example, if one wanted to make a string called "hello", they would have done the following:

```
char hello[6] = { 'h', 'e', 'l', 'l', 'o', '\0' };
```

Python, in its beautiful habit of maximum abstraction, keeps us from these complexities and lets us just declare:

```
hello = "hello"
```

The point is that strings, ultimately, are just sets of data. And like any set of data, they can be manipulated. There will be times, too, where we need to manipulate them.

The most simple form of string manipulation is the concept of concatenation. Concatenated strings are strings that are put together to form a new string. Concatenation is super easy - you simply use the + sign to literally add the strings together.

```
sentence = "My " + "grandmother " + "baked " + "today."
```

```
print sentence
#  would print "My grandmother
baked today."
```

The first thing to remember when working with string manipulation is that strings, like any set of data, starts counting at 0. So the string "backpack" would count like so:

b	a	c	k	p	a
c	k				
0	1	2	3	4	5
6	7				

There are a few different things that we can do with this knowledge alone. The first is that we can extract a single letter from it.

Let's say the string "backpack" were stored to a variable called *backpack*. We could extract the letter "p" from it by typing:

```
letter = backpack[4]
```

This would extract whatever the character at index 4 was in the string. Here, of course, it's *p*.

If we wanted to extract the characters from "b" to "p", we could do the following:

```
substring = backpack[ 0 : 4 ]
```

This would give the variable substring a string equal to the value of *backpack*'s 0 index to 4 index:

b	a	c	k	p	a
c	k				
0	*1*	*2*	*3*	*4*	*5*
6	7				

Substring, thus, would have the value of "backp". Quite the word.

There are a few more things you can do with data sets, and strings specifically, in order to get more specific results.

backpack[start:4] would give you all characters from the start to index four, like just before.

backpack[4:end] would give you all characters from index 4 to the end.

backpack[:2] would give you the first two characters, while backpack[-2:] would give you the last two characters. backpack[2:] would give you everything but the first two characters, while backpack[:-2] would give you everything aside from the last two characters.
However, it goes beyond this simple kind of arithmetic.

String variables also have built-in functions called methods. We've already worked with these a bit in the last chapter when we were working with files. Most things in Python - or object-oriented languages in general, really - are forms of things called objects. These are essentially variable types that have entire sets of properties associated with them. Macrovariables which contain a large number of microvariables and microfunctions, if you will.

Every single string is an instance of the *string* class, thus making it a string object. The string class contains definitions for methods which every string object can access, as an instance of the string class.

For example, let's create a bit of a heftier string.
tonguetwister = "Peter Piper picked a peck of pickled peppers"

The string class has a variety of built-in methods you can utilize in order to work with its objects.

Let's take the *split* method. If you were to type:

```
splitList = tonguetwister.split(' ')
```

It would split the sentence at every space, giving you a list of each word. splitList, thus, would look a bit like this: ['Peter', 'Piper', 'picked', 'a', 'peck', 'of', 'pickled', 'peppers']. Printing splitList[1] would give you the value 'Piper'.

There's also the *count* method, which would count the number of a certain character. Typing:

```
tonguetwister.lower().count('p')
```

You would get the number 9.

There's the *replace* method, which will replace a given string with another. For example, if you typed:

```
tonguetwister = tonguetwister.replace("peppers", "potatoes")
```

tonguetwister would now have the value of "Peter Piper picked a peck of pickled potatoes".

There's the *strip*, *lstrip*, and *rstrip* methods which take either a given character or whitespace off of both sides of the string. This is really useful when you're trying to parse user input. Unstripped user input can lead to unnecessarily large data sets and even buggy code.

The last major one is the *join* method, which will put a certain character between every character in the string.

```
print "-".join(tonguetwister)
```

would print "P-e-t-e-r-P-i-p-e-r-p-i-c-k-e-[...]"

There are also various boolean expressions which will return true or false. The startswith(*character*) and endswith(*character*) methods are two fantastic examples. If you were to type:

```
tonguetwister.startswith("P")
```

It would ultimately return true. However, if you were to type instead:

```
tonguetwister.startswith("H")
```

It would ultimately return false. These are used for internal evaluation of strings as well as for evaluating user input.

A few other examples are string.*isalnum()* which will see if all characters in the string are alphanumeric or if there are special characters, string.*isalpha()* which will see if all characters in the string are alphabetic, string.*isdigit()* which will check to see if the string is a digit or not, and string.*isspace()* which will check to see if the string is a space or not.

These are all extremely useful for parsing a given string and making determinations on what to do if the string is or isn't a certain way.

Chapter 8: Basic Object-Oriented Programming: Objects and Classes

Python is an object-oriented programming language. In fact, most modern languages are. But what exactly does this mean? We've spoken in vague terms of objects and classes but we haven't really established quite what this actually means in in any certain terms one way or another.

An object is an instance of a class. Most things you'll deal with in Python are objects. Earlier, when we worked with file input and output, we created instances of a file class. In the last chapter, we were working with strings, and we created instances of the string class. Every instance has built in methods that it can access that are derived from the class definition itself. So what exactly is a class?

A class is a way of defining objects. This sounds terribly vague, but let's look at it this way.

You likely have or have had a pet, right? Let's say there's a dog, and his name is Roscoe.

Well, Roscoe is an animal. Animals have broad, generally defined characteristics, but they're all animals, much like Roscoe is an animal. Get comfy with Roscoe, because we're going to be talking him a lot while we talk about the relations between classes and the relations between classes and objects.

We've established that Roscoe is *most certainly* an animal. He fits the definition of an animal. In this manner, Roscoe is a specific instance of the animal class. If you were writing a simulation of life, and you had people and animals, you would define Roscoe as an instance of *animal,* just as you declared variable *file1* as an instance of *file,* or you declared *tonguetwister* as an instance of *string.*

Now, we need to talk about how we actually define a class and an object within Python.

Create a new file to work with, I'm calling mine pursuitOfRoscoe.py.

Within this file, we're going to start right out the bat by defining a class.

To declare a class, you follow the following template:

```
class name(parent)
```

We'll talk about parent classes in the next chapter. For now, let's just make our animal class. Every class which isn't deriving from another class has "object" as its parent, so let's put that.

```
class Animal(object):
```

We're on our way to defining Roscoe, now. We need a way to define an animal. Let's think about what most animals have. Most animals have legs, that's a start. Animals also have Latin names. Let's work with those two. If your class stores data, you generally need to have an initializer function within your class. It's not a necessity, but it is very common practice.

```
class Animal(object):
    def __init__(self, legs, name):
        self.legs = legs
        self.name = name
```

Perfect. Since Roscoe's a dog, he'll have 4 legs, and his species is Canis Lupus Familiaris.

With that in mind, we now have a definition for animal classes that can be used amongst many animals, not just Roscoe. That's the entire idea behind classes: creating reusable data structures for any given object so that the code is more readable, easy to understand, cleaner, and portable, among other buzzword adjectives that are surprisingly very, very true.

How do we declare an instance of this class now? Like anything else!

```
roscoe = Animal(4, "Canis Lupus Familiaris")
```

We can go in and change these variables too. Canis lupus is so formal, and Roscoe's our buddy, so let's change that to Roscoe.

```
roscoe.name = "Roscoe"
```

There we go. *Much* better.

Hopefully, this makes the distinction between classes and objects *much* clearer.

Roscoe is a dog, and an animal. Thus he takes from the common concept of being an animal. Since he's an instance of an animal, he automatically receives the traits that all animals have. How cool is that?

Let's go a bit further, and incorporate some functions. What's something that every animal does? Sleep. Every single animal sleeps, aside from Ozzy Osborne.

Let's give animals a function so that they can sleep.

Below our initializer, create a new function called sleep that takes the arguments of *self* and *hours*. Then print out a line of text that says the animal's name and how long it's sleeping for. My code ended up looking a bit like this, and hopefully yours will as well.

```
def sleep(self, hours):
    print "%s is sleeping for %d hours!" % (self.name, hours)
```

Then below our declaration of Roscoe, let's go ahead and run the "sleep" function with the argument of 4 hours.

```
roscoe = Animal(4, "canis lupus familiaris")
roscoe.name = "Roscoe"
roscoe.sleep(4)
```

Save this and run it. If all goes well, it should print out "Roscoe is sleeping for 4 hours!".

At this point you've got a cursory understanding of classes. We'll go more in-depth with broad object oriented programming concepts and their applicability within Python in the next chapter.

Chapter 9: More on Object-Oriented Programming and Classes

There are a few very broad object-oriented concepts we've yet to cover, and this is because they require a far more in-depth explanation than I was willing to give in the same exact chapter that we began to talk about any of the concepts.

There are four primary concepts within object-oriented programming that we need to discuss more in-depth. These are inheritance, polymorphism, abstraction, and encapsulation. Python provides for all of these, and very well at that.

Inheritance is the notion of deriving a class and things from within that class into another child class. There's a very simple way to explain this concept. Classes can break down into other more specific classes. For example, Roscoe is an animal. But he's also a dog. A dog is a type of animal. Shouldn't Roscoe be a dog and not an animal? Isn't he both? How do we handle this?

Think of it this way: every dog is an animal, but not every animal is a dog. So we can break down the animal class even further. The way that we derive one class from another is by *inheritance*. Here's how we'd declare a dog class which extends the animal class. All dogs have 4 legs aside (for the most part), so we can declare that ahead of time and manually change it if a dog ever doesn't have 4 legs.

```
class Dog(Animal):
    def __init__(self, name):
        self.name = name
        self.legs = 4
```

The way that this works is that the Dog class is an extension of the Animal class. The Dog class receives all the functions and variables of the dog class, so we don't have to redefine them.

This also means that if we were to erase our first line and re-declare Roscoe more accurately as a dog, we could still declare *sleep*. Observe.

```
roscoe = Dog("Roscoe")
roscoe.sleep(4)
```

It should go without a hitch. However, the cool thing about child classes is that you can also give them their own functions that their parent can't use. For example, animals don't bark - dogs do. Let's create a bark function in our dog class for practice's sake.

```
def bark(self):
    "%s says: Bark!" % self.name
```

Now let's try to declare bark via Roscoe.

```
roscoe.bark()
```

It should print out exactly what we entered. To illustrate further, create an instance of parent class Animal, let's call it "lion":

```
lion = Animal(4, "panthera leo")
```

Try to call the method *bark* by way of Lion.

```
lion.bark()
```

There should be an error. Why is this? Well, it's because - as we said - every dog is an animal, but not every animal is a dog. The *bark*() function was defined in the Dog class but not in the Animal class, so instances of the Animal class can't access this method at all.

The next concept of object-oriented programming is called "polymorphism". This means that something has the property of being able to perform the same task as something else, but in a different way. There are two ways of achieving this: function *overloading* (performing a similar function/method but with different parameters) and function *overriding* (rewriting a function of a parent class so that it works better for your own class).

To illustrate this, let's go back to our bark method. Under our bark method, we're going to create another bark method, declared like this:

```
def bark(number):
    print "%s just barked, %d times! How cute." % (self.name, number)
```

Now we have two different forms of the bark function. If you declare

```
roscoe.bark()
```

You're going to see "Roscoe says: Bark!"

But, if you declare

```
roscoe.bark(3)
```

You'll see "Roscoe just barked, 3 times! How cute."

This is the basic idea of function overloading and polymorphism in essence: giving multiple ways to do a similar thing.

This program is already adorable, but we can make it even more adorable while also learning more about Python coding and string manipulation. Go back to your *bark(number)* method, and change it so it looks like this:

```
barkString = "Bark! " * number
    print "%s just barked, %d times. How cute. %s) (self.name, number, barkString)
```

Now save and run. You can repeat a string multiple times by simply using the multiplication and giving how many times to multiply!

The next major concept of object-oriented programming languages is *abstraction*. This is the idea of hiding internal details and functionality, to be more forward and more safe for both the programmer and end user. Python shows this by having a very abstract interface compared to other languages and providing a large amount of functionality for you so you never have to get down to the nitty-gritty of what your computer is actually doing behind the scenes.

The last major concept of object-oriented languages is called *encapsulation*, wherein code and data is wrapped together into a single unit. The primary way that we can display this is by the notion of having a class - not only in Python, but anywhere. Using a class automatically wraps important data and functions together in one easily accessible and usable place. Other datas have something called *access control* where you can actually dictate what classes can and can't access the data that you're putting in your class. Class data in Python is by default public.

All in all, object-oriented programming isn't very tough to grasp, but it's full of concepts that stand for much bigger and larger things, and these are the concepts that can be difficult to understand and implement in the end.

Now we're going to incorporate the concepts we've been going over in the past few chapters - string manipulation, file input/output, and classes - in the next one as a final way to work on and put together all of the concepts we've built up so far, making a program that will keep a list of books for the end user.

Chapter 10: Book List Redux

Congrats on making it this far. Programming is confusing at first. Now it's time to combine the concepts we've learned and create a newer version of our book list program.

So let's think about what we want this program to do.

I want this program to have five options:

1) Add books to a temporary list
2) List the temporary book list
3) Read books from a file
4) Write the temporary list to a new book file
5) Write it to an existing file
6) Clear the temporary list.

So let's get started with this.

Let's create a new file, I'm calling it bookkeeper.py, because I'm a programmer in 2016 and the modus operandi is using trendy catchy names.

In this file, the first thing we want to do is create a class called book.

```
class book(object):
    def __init__(self, title, author):
        self.title = title
        self.author = author
```

Now we need to start making our functions. The first function, addBook, is going to create a new instance of the book class and add it to our list of books.

```
def addBook(bookList):
    title = raw_input("What is the name of the book?")
    author = raw_input("What is the author's name?")
    bookList.append(book(title.upper(), author.title()))
```

The reason that we put author.title() is because the *string*.title() method manipulates a string such that every first word is capitalized, much like a title.

Afterwards, we need a function in order to list the books. We'll pass to it a list of books.

```
def listBook(bookList):
    for i in bookList:
        print "\"%s\", by %s\n" % (i.title, i.author)
```

This will loop through every book in book list and print out their title and author, accessing their respective properties.

This is where things get pretty fun. We need to create a function in order to read books from a file. Additionally, we're going to give people the option to add it to their temporary book list. We'll start by declaring the function and then passing the list of books.

```
def readBooks(bookList):
```

Then we're going to declare a second temporary list within the function that we're going to save every book in the file to.

```
bList = []
```

After this, we open the file for reading. We need to prompt the user for the filename. We'll do that like so:

```
f = open(raw_input(" Enter the filename."))
```

Now, we're going to iterate through every line in this file. There's a handy built-in functionality for this in Python using for loops. We're going to then use our string method *string*.find() in order to locate the comma in the line and divide the line of text there into a title and an author, by creating two substrings. Each of these substrings will need to be stripped - the first of the comma, and the second of whitespace. After this, we're going to append the book to the function's book list, printing out each line as we go. A bit of a complicated set of code, but it'll explain itself.

```
for line in f:
    comma = line.find(",")
    title = line[0:comma].rstrip(',') #substring 1
    author = line[comma+1:].strip() #substring 2
    bList.append(book(title.upper(), author.title()))
    print "%s, %s" % (title.upper(), author.title())
```

Next, we prompt the user, asking if they want to add the results to their temporary list. If they say yes, we iterate through bList, appending each book to bookList. Otherwise, we just tell them it wasn't saved and close the file.

```
if userInput == "yes":
        for i in bList:
                bookList.append(i)
        print "Saved."
else:
        print "Not saved."
f.close()
```

That brings an end to our readBooks method.

Now it's time to get to our writeToNew method.

First we define it, then ask the user to name the file. We then open the file, iterate through a book list while writing the contents to that file, then close it.

```
def writeToNew(bookList):
        userInput = raw_input(" Enter the filename you'd like to export to.")
        f = open(userInput, 'w') # the w indicates that we'd like to write
        for i in bookList:
                f.write("%s, %s\n" % (i.title.upper(), i.author.title()))
        f.close()
```

Now we need to create the "write to existing file" method. It's simple enough.

Ultimately, it's very similar to the last function, but we change an essential argument.

```
def writeToExisting(bookList):
    userInput = raw_input(" Enter the file you'd like to add to.")
    f = open(userInput, 'a') # using a instead of w tells it we'll be appending a file, rather than writing a new one
    for i in bookList:
        f.write("%s, %s\n" % (i.title.upper(), i.author.title()))
```

Those are the primary functions that needed to be written. Now it's time to move on to the actual bulk of our code.

First we define our bookList and our running boolean.

```
bookList = []
running = True
```

Now we start our while loop. The last program was very messy. Let's clean it up a bit.

First, we're going to create a much prettier menu:

```
while running == True:
    print "Welcome to BOOKKEEPER. Type:"
    print "\t\"ADD\" to add a book to your temp list."
    print"\t\"LIST\" to read out your temp list."
    print "\t\"READ\" to read an existing file."
```

```
            print "\t\"SAVE NEW\" to save
to a new file."
            print "\t\"SAVE EXISTING\" to
save to an existing file."
            print "\t\"CLEAR\" to clear
your temporary list."
            print "\t\"EXIT\" to exit."
```

Already, our menu is looking much prettier and more organized than it was. A tab space before each option really spruces it up. Now it's time to actually accept the user input and make decisions. You simply call every function, sending them bookList, until you get to the "clear" option. When you get to the "clear" variation, you've simply got to reset bookList to be empty by re-declaring it as empty. This is really pretty straightforward.

```
        userInput = raw_input()
        if userInput.lower() == "add":
            addBook(bookList)
        elif userInput.lower() == "list":
            listBook(bookList)
        elif userInput.lower() == "read":
            readBooks(bookList)
        elif userInput.lower() == "save new":
            writeToNew(bookList)
        elif userInput.lower() == "save existing":
            writeToExisting(bookList)
        elif userInput.lower() == "clear":
            bookList = []
        elif userInput.lower() == "exit":
            running = False
        else:
            print "The command was invalid!\n\n"
```

That brings an end to our program. It's far easier to understand and grasp than the former, and is far more fleshed out. Python is pretty forgiving structurally, but just to be sure, here's how the program looks for me. Feel free to compare yours:

```
class book(object):
    def __init__(self, title, author):
        self.title = title
        self.author = author

def addBook(bookList):
    title = raw_input("What is the name of the book?")
    author = raw_input("What is the author's name?")

    bookList.append(book(title.upper(), author.title()))

def listBook(bookList):
    for i in bookList:
        print "\"%s\", by %s\n" % (i.title.upper(), i.author)

def readBooks(bookList):
    bList = []
    f = open(raw_input(" Enter the filename."))
    for line in f:
        comma = line.find(",")
        title = line[0:comma].rstrip(',')
        author = line[comma+1:].strip()

        bList.append(book(title.upper(), author.title()))
        print "%s, %s" % (title.upper(), author.title())
```

```
        userInput = raw_input("Would
you like to record this to your
temporary list?")
        if userInput == "yes":
            for i in bList:
                bookList.append(i)
            print "Saved."
        else:
            print "Not saved."
        f.close()

def writeToNew(bookList):
    userInput = raw_input("Enter
the filename you'd like to export
to.")
    f = open(userInput, 'w')
    for i in bookList:
        f.write("%s, %s\n" %
(i.title.upper(),
i.author.title()))
    f.close()

def writeToExisting(bookList):
    userInput = raw_input("Enter
the filename you'd like to add
to.")
    f = open(userInput, 'a')
    for i in bookList:
        f.write("%s, %s\n" %
(i.title.upper(),
i.author.title()))
    f.close()

bookList = []
running = True

while running == True:
    print "Welcome to BOOKKEEPER.
Type:"
    print "\t\"ADD\" to add a book
to your temp list."
    print "\t\"LIST\" to read out
your temp list."
```

```
        print "\t\"READ\" to read an 
existing file."
        print "\t\"SAVE NEW\" to save 
to a new file."
        print "\t\"SAVE EXISTING\" to 
save to an existing file."
        print "\t\"CLEAR\" to clear 
your temporary list."
        print "\t\"EXIT\" to exit."
        userInput = raw_input()
        if userInput.lower() == "add":
            addBook(bookList)
        elif userInput.lower() == 
"list":
            listBook(bookList)
        elif userInput.lower() == 
"read":
            readBooks(bookList)
        elif userInput.lower() == "save 
new":
            writeToNew(bookList)
        elif userInput.lower() == "save 
existing":
            writeToExisting(bookList)
        elif userInput.lower() == 
"clear":
            bookList = []
        elif userInput.lower() == 
"exit":
            running = False
        else:
            print "The command was 
invalid!\n\n"
```

This program has hopefully helped you to understand how we can synthesize a lot of the concepts that we've covered so far. I also hope that it helped you to understand a bit more the relation between classes and objects. There are certainly far more confusing things in the language, but object-oriented concepts as such can be a little difficult to comprehend anyway.

      Having gone through the major concepts and facets of the language, we've covered the bulk of the important things that there are to cover. At this point, I'd like to drive home how important of a resource the internet can be. Programming can be something that will make you want to tear your hair out at times. Admittedly, Python is an easier language, and even better, the compiler can be very informational, especially compared to other languages such as C++ or C where the compiler can be very confusing.

      There will always be something you don't know in the world of programming, and when you're starting out, the list is endless. For practical purposes, there's only so much that I can cover in the relatively limited scope of a beginner book. However, there are also more answers than you can ever imagine. The beautiful thing about programming is that everything has a solution somewhere. Often, it'll already be developed in an API or module somewhere. When it's not, it's ultimately possible. The beauty of programming is that it's an incredible way to express yourself, and if something can be done, it can be done on a computer. Computers break down in a very, very simple way to sequences of 1s and 0s and computations that are performed constantly, but in that simplicity is an endless amount of extrapolated complexity.

We may have written a relatively simple program. But the concepts contained therein will underlie a lot of the concepts that you may work with going forward while working with any other program or programming language.

And at the end of the day, if nothing else, you can say that you've written a really cool program to help you keep track of any and all books that you own, including this one. Isn't that really a victory in and of itself?

Conclusion

Thank you for making it through to the end of the *book*, let's hope it was informative and able to provide you with all of the tools you need to achieve your goals whatever they may be.

The next step is to use this knowledge to your advantage. Do something with it. You can absolutely use this book as a reference, but it wasn't written to necessarily be one - this book was written in order to teach you the essence of programming and everything that you need to do to start programming in Python, as well as the essential tools of the language that you'll have to know how to use as a beginner.

Python has a ton of support and is immensely popular, so you can find a way to use it for whatever you may need to do. For example, for game programming, there is the PyGame library.

Ultimately this book was written with the goal in mind of teaching you not necessarily about Python, but programming at large. Programming is a science, yet it is also an art - it's a form of self-expression, of manipulating computer bytecode in order to get the end result you desire out of your brain and onto the computer screen. Python is just one means by which you can accomplish this goal.

Python is ultimately derived from a language called C, and the C programming language would go onto inspire a huge number of languages - not only Python, but also C++, Java, Lua, Go, D, R, Ruby, and so many more. This book was intended to teach you the underlying concepts so that you're not restricted by any given programming language, because programming languages are much the same across one or another. The important thing is that you understand the underlying concepts - control flow, objects, input and output, manipulating variables - so that you can produce the end result that you want.

So with all of that said, if you found this book useful in anyway, a review on Amazon is always appreciated. I hope you found this book to be a useful and fantastic starting place as a Python learner and hopeful programmer, whether you're programming for your career or programming simply as a hobby.

Python:

Best Practices to Programming Code with Python

Charlie Masterson

Introduction

I want to thank you and congratulate you for reading the book, "Python: Best Practices to Programming Code with Python". This book contains proven steps and strategies on how to program in Python more effectively. When you first learn Python, you will be taught how to write code, but in many cases, you will not be taught how to write that code neatly.

If you speak to any Python programmer, ask them what it is they like about Python. I guarantee they will tell you that one of the main reasons is because it is easily readable. In fact, this is the absolute heart of the Python language, simply because computer code is read far more than it is written. Much of this is down to the fact that Python code follows a set of guidelines and "Pythonic" idioms – if you hear a programmer refer to a part of the code as not being "Pythonic", it means that it doesn't follow those guidelines and it doesn't express intent in any readable manner.

Code style and layout is incredibly important, as is consistency in the style that you use. With that said, there are times when consistency isn't the right thing and the guidelines are simply not applicable – you have to know when that time is and that is when best judgment comes into programming with Python.

With this guide, I am going to show you the absolute best way to write your code, tidying up your program and making it all more effective and efficient. I won't just give you the basic. I will delve deep into everything you need to know, from the layout of the code to how to write functions, idioms, and names.

I will talk about whitespaces and tabs, strings, and methods. I will also be giving you some general recommendations for Python programming along with the general concepts. In short, by the time you have read my Best Practice guide, you will be the best Python programmer you can possibly be.

My book does assume some prior knowledge of Python programming, so if you are a complete newbie to the programming scene, please familiarize yourself with Python code before you read this book. My aim is to help you to produce Python code that is free from, or at least has very few, complications or obvious problems, as well as making it more readable for others.

Thanks again for reading this book, I hope you enjoy it!

Chapter 1: General Concepts of Python Coding

Before we get properly into the book, these are the general concepts of coding that you should be aware of; concepts that will make life easier for you.

Explicit Code

While you can do all sorts of weird and wonderful things with Python, it is best to keep it straightforward and explicit.

A Bad Example:
```
def make_complex(*args):
    x, y = args
    return dict(**locals())
```

A Good Example:
```
def make_complex(x, y):
    return {'x': x, 'y': y}
```

Compare these examples; in the latter example of code, we explicitly received **x** and **y** from the caller and the return is an explicit dictionary.

The developer who wrote this knows what to do just by looking at the first line and the last line; this is not the case with the bad example.

One Line, One Statement

While there are compound statements, like the list comprehensions, that are allowed and, in many cases, appreciated, it is not good practice to have 2 statements that are disjointed on one code line.

A Bad Example:
```
print 'one'; print 'two'

if x == 1: print 'one'

if <complex comparison> and <other
complex comparison>:
    # do something
```

A Good Example:
```
print 'one'
print 'two'

if x == 1:
    print 'one'

cond1 = <complex comparison>
cond2 = <other complex comparison>
if cond1 and cond2:
    # do something
```

Returning Values

When you get a function that is ever-growing in complexity, it isn't unheard of to use several return statements in the body of the function. However, if you want to maintain clear intent and a good level of readability, you should try not to return values from several points in the function body.

When it comes to returning values within a function, there are 2 cases for doing so: the result that comes from a normally processed function return, and the errors that are indicative of incorrect input parameters or for any reason that the function cannot complete the computation.

If you don't want exceptions raised for the latter case, then it might be necessary for values, such as False or None to be returned, as an indication that the function was not able to perform properly. In cases such as this, it is best practice to return as soon as the wrong context has been noticed.

This will help to neaten up the function structure because all code that comes after the error return assumes that the condition has been met so that the main function result can be computed. As such, it is sometimes necessary to have several return statements like this.

That said, if a function contains several different courses it can go, it can be unwieldy to debug the result so it is preferable to maintain just one course. This also helps in working out code paths and, if you have several courses, it could be an indication that you need to re-look at your code and tidy it up.

For Example:

```
def complex_function(c, b, a):
    if not c:
        return None  # Raising an exception might be better
    if not b:
        return None  # Raising an exception might be better
    # Some elaborate code that is trying to make x from c, b and a
    # Try not to return x if successful
    if not x:
        # A Plan-B calculation of x
    return x  # One exit point for the value x will be helpful
              # when trying to maintain the code.t
```

Chapter 2: Programming Recommendations

These are the basic recommendations for writing Python code, recommendations that you should follow if your code is going to be more effective and efficient as well as being readable.

- Your code must be written so that it doesn't disadvantage other Python implementations, such as **IronPython, Jython, PyPy, Psyco and Cython.**

For example, you should never rely on the efficient string concatenation of CPython that takes the form of `a=a+b` or `a+=b`. This is a somewhat fragile optimization, even though it super-efficient in CPython, because it won't work on al type sand it won't be present in any Python implementation that does not use refcounting.

Instead, where you use a part of the library that is performance-sensitive, you should use the `.join()` form instead. This will make sure that the concatenation is linear across all the different Python implementations.

- Never use an equality operator to make comparisons to a singleton such as None. Instead, use `is` or `not`.

You should also be wary of using `if x` when really you should be using `if is not None`. An example of this is when you are testing if an argument or a variable that defaults to a value of None was actually set to a different value. The other value could have a type that is false in the Boolean context.

- Rather than using the operator `not is`, you should use `is not`. While they both are identical in terms of function, the first is low on the readability scale, making the second one more preferable. An example:

Use This:
`if foo is not None:`

Don't Use This:
`if not foo is None`

- When you implement an ordering operation with a rich comparison, you should implement all of the 6 operations instead of relying on some other code to exercise a comparison. Those operations are (`__eq__`, `__lt__`, `__ne__`, `__ge__`, `__gt__`, `__le__`)

To cut down on the effort needed, one particular decorator helps to generate any comparison methods that are missing. That decorator is `functools.total_ordering()`.

The style guidelines indicate that Python assumes reflexivity rules. As such, the Python interpreter might change things about by swapping `y > x` with `x < y`, or it may swap `y >= x` with `x <= y`.

You may also find that the argument `x == y` has been swapped with `x != y`. The `min()` and `sort()` operations will also definitely use the `<` operator and the `max()` function will use the `>`operator. However, you should, as a best practice guide, use all of them so that there is no confusion.

- Rather than using an assignment statement that will bind a lambda expression to an identifier, use a `def` statement

A Good Example:
```
def f(x): return 2*x
```

A Bad Example:
```
f = lambda x: 2*x
```

The first example shows that the name given to the function object is 'f' rather than the collective <lambda>. This is the most useful for string representations and for tracebacks and, by using the assignment statement, you cut out the one benefit that a lambda expression offers over and above a def statement – that it may be embedded within a bigger statement.

When you want to derive exceptions, use Exception and not BaseException. Inheritance from the latter is reserved for those exceptions where it is pretty much always wrong to catch them

When you design your exception hierarchies, base them on the quality that is likely to be needed by catching exceptions, rather than on the location where the exception is raised. Always answer one question – "what has gone wrong?" rather than just saying that something is wrong. Use the conventions for class naming but do remember to add the "Error" suffix to the exception classes that produce an error.

There is no need to put any special suffixes on exceptions that are not errors and are used as flow-control or another form of signaling.

- When you use exception chaining, use it only where needed.

When you replace an inner exception deliberately, make sure that the right details are relocated into the newer exception. Examples of this are making sure the name of the attribute is preserved when you convert `KeyError` to `Attribute Error` or when you embed the original exception text into the message in the newer exception

- When using Python 2 and you raise an exception, always use the `raise ValueError)'message')` instead of `raise ValueError 'message'`

This is because the second example is neither valid nor legal syntax for Python 3. Also, the use of the containing parentheses means that there is no requirement to use continuation characters on a line when you add string formatting or when an exception argument is too long.

- When you catch exceptions, always mention specific ones wherever you can rather than using the bare except: clause

For Example:

```
try:
    import platform_specific_module
except ImportError:
    platform_specific_module = None
```

`KeyboardInterrupt` and `SystemExit` exceptions will be caught by a bare except: clause and this makes it much more difficult to interrupt programs using CTRL+C and they can also cover up other problems that may be there.

If you are looking to catch every exception that signals errors in the program, use except Exception:

A general rule is to only use the bare except: clause in one of these two cases:

1. If the traceback is being printed by the exception handler; that way, the user will be made aware of any errors

2. If cleanup work is needed but the code allows the exception to propagate up using raise. A more efficient way to do this would be to use `try...finally`.

When you are binding a caught exception to a name, use the explicit binding syntax from Python 2.6:

```
try:
    process_data()
except Exception as exc:
    raise DataProcessingFailedError(str(exc))
```

This is the ONLY syntax that Python 3 supports and it cuts out any problems of ambiguity that are associated with the older-style syntax that is comma-based.

- When you are catching system errors, use the exception hierarchy from Python 3.3 rather than errno values. As well, when you use any try/except clause, try to limit the use of the try clause to the least amount of code. This will cut down the risk of errors being hidden

A Good Example:
```
try:
    value = collection[key]
except KeyError:
    return key_not_found(key)
else:
    return handle_value(value)
```

A Bad Example:
```
try:
    # Too broad!
    return handle_value(collection[key])
except KeyError:
    # Will catch a KeyError that is raised by handle_value()
    return key_not_found(key)
```

- When you use a resource tool that is local to a specific code section, use it with a statement to make sure that it is cleaned immediately after use. You can also use a try/finally statement

- Always invoke a context manager through separate methods or functions whenever they are for a purpose other than getting and releasing resources.

A Good Example:
```
with conn.start_transaction():
    do_something_in_transaction(conn)
```

A Bad Example:

```
with conn:
    do_something_in_transaction(conn)
```

The second example does not give us any information that indicates whether the __enter__ and __exit__ methods do anything other than shutting the transaction. In this case, it is important to be explicit.

- Consistency in return statements is important. Either all of the function return statements or none of the return statements should return an expression or value. If a return statement does return an expression, any that do not return any value should state explicitly that the return is None and there should be a return statement at the end of that function

A Good Example:
```
def foo(x):
    if x >= 0:
        return math.sqrt(x)
    else:
        return None

def bar(x):
    if x < 0:
        return None
    return math.sqrt(x)
```

A Bad Example:
```
def foo(x):
```

```
    if x >= 0:
        return math.sqrt(x)

def bar(x):
    if x < 0:
        return
    return math.sqrt(x)
```

- Don't use string modules; use string methods instead

These are always faster and they share an API with the Unicode strings. This rule can be ignored if you need backward compatibility with a Python implementation that is earlier than 2.0

- Instead of using string slicing as a way of checking for suffixes and prefixes, use ``.startswith()`` and ``.endswith()`` instead

These are much cleaner methods and they are less prone to errors.

A Good Example:
```
if foo.beginswith('bar'):
```

A Bad Example:
```
if foo[:3] == 'bar':
```

- When you are comparing object types, use `isinstance()` instead of direct comparisons

A Good Example:
```
if isinstance(obj, int):
```

A Bad Example:
```
if type(obj) is type(1):
```

When you check to see if an object is actually a string, remember that it could be a Unicode string as well. In Python 2.0, Unicode and str share the base class called `basestring` so you could do:

```
if isinstance(obj, basestring):
```

However, in Python 3, you won't find basestring or Unicode, only str and bytes objects are not strings anymore, they are integer sequences instead.

For a sequence – tuples, lists, strings, etc. – make use of the fact that an empty sequence is false.

A Good Example:
```
if not seq:
    if seq:
```

A Bad Example:
```
if len(seq):
```

```
if not len(seq):
```

Don't include any string literals that require significant levels of trailing whitespace because this is not distinguishable and some text editors will remove them

Don't use == to compare a Boolean value to True or False:

A Good Example:
```
if greeting:
```

A Bad Example:
```
if the greeting == True:
```

An Even Worse Example:
```
if the greeting is True:
```

Chapter 3: Code Layout

The most obvious place to start with is how to layout your code. I will be giving you the best practice guidelines for code layout along with examples on how to do it and how not to:

Indentation and Alignment

Every indent level should be 4 spaces.

When you use continuation lines, they should align the wrapped elements using one of two methods:

- Vertically with the Python implicit way of joining lines inside braces, brackets, and parentheses, or

- With hanging indents

When you use a hanging indent, consider that there shouldn't be any arguments on line one and that, to mark the continuation line, indentation must be used.

Consider the following examples:

The Right Way:
```
# Aligned with an opening delimiter.
foo     =      long_function_name(var_four,
var_three,
                         var_two,
var_one)
```

```
# and some more indentation included so
this is distinguished from the rest of
the code

def long_function_name(
        var_four, var_three, var_two,
        var_one):
    print(var_four)

# Hanging indents should be used to add a
level.
foo = long_function_name(
    var_four, var_three,
    var_two, var_one)
```

The Wrong Way:
```
# Arguments on first line are forbidden
when you are not using vertical
alignment.
foo   =    long_function_name(var_four,
var_three,
    var_two, var_one)

# More indentation is required as the
indentation is not distinguishable from
the rest.
def long_function_name(
    var_four, var_three, var_two,
    var_one):
    print(var_four)
```

When it comes to continuation lines, the rule on 4 indent spaces is optional:

```
# it is possible for hanging indents *to*
be indented to more or less than 4
spaces.
```

```
foo = long_function_name(
  var_four, var_three,
  var_two, var_one)
```

When you use an if-statement with a long condition that can be written over more than one line, note that there is an easy to create a natural indent of 4 spaces for the rest of the lines in the conditional – use a keyword of 2 characters (for example, if) along with one space and an opening parenthesis. However, visually, this can look like some kind of incompatibility with the indented code within the if-statement, which will already have a 4-space indent. There is no real position on whether to distinguish these conditional lines from the code inside the nest but there are a few acceptable options you can use, including but not limited to:

```
# No extra indentation used.
if (this_is_one_thing and
    that_is_something_else):
    do_this()
```

```
# Add a comment, which will provide some help in the editors
# supporting highlighting of syntax.
if (this_is_one_thing and
    that_is_something_else):
    # as both conditions are true, we can tweak.
    do_this()
```

```
# Add more indentation to the conditional
continuation line.
if (this_is_one_thing
        and that_is_something_else):
    do_this()
```

Now, when you have a construction of multiple lines, the closing brace, parentheses, or bracket can line up in one of two places – either beneath the beginning character that is NOT a white space on the end line of the list:

```
my_list = [
    6, 5, 4,
    3, 2, 1,
    ]
result = a_function_that_will_take_arguments(
    'f', 'e', 'd',
    'c', 'b', 'a',
    )
```

Or it can be lined up beneath the beginning character of the first line in the multiple line construction:

```
my_list = [
    6, 5, 4,
    3, 2, 1,
]
result = a_function_that_will_take_arguments(
    'f', 'e', 'd',
    'c', 'b', 'a',
)
```

Chapter 4: Idioms

Programming idioms are, in simple terms, the way in which Python code should be written. We often refer to idiomatic code as Pythonic code and, although there tends to be one very obvious way to write something, the actual way in which Pythonic code is written can be a bit obscure to those who are new to Python. So, you need to learn good idioms and some of the more common ones are:

Unpacking

Provided you know how long a tuple or list is, unpacking allows you to give each element a name. For example, `enumerate()` gives us a tuple with 2 elements for each of the items in the list:

```
for the index, each item in enumerate(this_list):
    # do something with the index and each item
```

You can also use unpacking to swap the variables:

```
b, a = a, b
```

And you can use nested unpacking:

```
c, (b, a) = 3, (2, 1)
```

When Python 3 was implemented, it came with a new extended unpacking method:

```
c *the_rest = [3, 2, 1]
# c = 3, the_rest = [2, 1]
c, *the_middle, c = [4, 3, 2, 1]
# c = 4, the_middle = [3, 2], c = 1
```

Creating Ignored Variables

If you wanted to assign something but do not need to use the variable, you would use ___. For example:

```
filename = 'footbar.txt'
basename,       _,       ext       = filename.rpartition('.')
```

NOTE
You will often see it recommended that you use a single underscore (_) for variables that are throwaway, rather than using a double underscore(__). The problem with this is, "-", the single underscore, tends to be used in the `gettext()` function as an alias. It is also used to store the value of the previous operation at the interactive prompt. When you use a double underscore, "__", it is clear and it is convenient. It also cuts out the accidental risk of interfering with the other use cases of the single underscore.

Creating Length-N Lists

To create a length-N list that is of the same thing, you would use the * list operator

```
four_zeros = [Zero] * 4
```

To create a length-N list of a list you should not use the * operator. That operator creates lists of N that refer to the same list and that is not what we want here. Instead, we use a list comprehension:

```
four_lists = [[] for __ in xrange(4)]
```

Note – If you are using Python 3, use **range()** and not **xrange()**

Creating Strings from Lists

The most common idiom for creating strings is **str.join()** on empty strings:

```
letters = ['c', 'l', o, 't']
word = ''.join(letters)
```

This sets a value of "clot" to the variable *word*. You can apply this idiom to tuples and lists.

Searching a Collection for an Item

On occasion, you will need to search a collection for a specific option and there are two ways to do this – using lists or sets

Look at this example:

```
s = set(['c', 'l', 'o', 't'])
l = ['c', 'l', 'o', 't']
```

```
def lookup_set(s):
    return 's' in s

def lookup_list(l):
    return 's' in l
```

Now, both of these functions look exactly the same simply because `lookup_set` uses that fact that Python sets are hash tables. However, the performance of `lookup` in each of the examples is different. In order to decide whether a specific item is contained in a list, Python has to search through every single item until it finds one that matches. This takes time, especially if you have a long list. With sets, each item has a hash that tells Python where to look for the matching item. This makes the search much quicker even if the sets are big ones. You can also search dictionaries in the same way. Because there is a difference in the performance, it is a better idea to use a set or a dictionary rather than a list in the following cases:

- Where a collection contains a lot of items

- Where you are going to be searching for items in a collection on a repeated basis

- There are no duplicate items

In cases of smaller collections or those that you are not likely to be searching on a frequent basis, the extra memory and time needed to set the hash table up will, more often than not, be more than the time you save by improving the speed of the search

Chapter 5: Comments

Because you already have some experience of Python coding, you will know that a comment is invisible when the program is run. A comment is there to help the coder and others who read it to understand what has been done and why. Now, some people think that, because they are invisible then there is no need to write them while others write comments that make no sense and that contradict their code. I have to tell you that, out of the two, having a contradictory comment is far worse than not writing one at all and, as such, whenever you make changes to your code, you must make sure that you update your comments.

When you write a comment, ensure that it is a proper sentence with a proper ending. As it is when you write anything, your comment, be it a sentence or a phrase, must have a capital letter to start it. The only exception to that rule is if it is an identifier that starts with a lower-case letter – a golden rule here is that you NEVER change the case of an identifier!

If you are using a short comment you can leave off the full-stop at the end. If you are writing block comments, these tend to be made up of at least one paragraph, sometimes more, each one built from whole sentences. Each of these sentences must have a full-stop. Following each full-stop there should be 2 spaces and all comments should be written in English. The only exception to this is if you are 200% certain that your code is never going to be read by people who do not speak or read your language

Block Comments:

A block comment tends to apply to some or all of the code that comes after it. The comment should be indented in the exact same way as the code it refers to and each line of each block must begin with a # and one space. The only exception is if you have used indented text within the comment. All paragraphs in each block comment must be separated with a line that contains one #.

Inline Comments

These should be used as little as possible. As a refresher, an inline comment is a comment that is placed on the same line that a statement is on. An inline comment has to be separated from the statement by a minimum of two spaces and they must begin with one # and one space.

In all honesty, you should avoid using inline comments because they are not really necessary and can cause an unwanted distraction.

For example, you should never do this:

```
x = x + 1                 # Increment x
```

However, sometimes, this could be useful:

```
x = x + 1                    # Compensate
for the border
```

Chapter 6: Conventions

To make your Python code much read better, follow these conventions:

Look to see if your variables are equal to a constant. There is no need for an explicit comparison of the values to 0, None or True; instead, you could add it into the if-statement. Look at the following examples:

A Bad Example:
```
if attr == True:
    print 'True!'

if attr == None:
    print 'attr is None!'
```

A Good Example:
```
# Just look at the value
if attr:
    print 'attr is the best!'

# or check to see what the opposite is
if not attr:
    print 'attr is the worst!'

# or, as None is considered to be false,
make you sure you run an explicit check
for it
if attr is None:
    print 'attr is None!'
```

How to Access Dictionary Elements:

Instead of using the method **dict.has-key()**, use the syntax, **x in d** or use **dict.get()** to pass default arguments to.

A Bad Example:
```
d = {'hello': 'world'}
if d.has_key('hello'):
    print d['hello']    # prints 'world'
else:
    print 'the_default_value'
```

A Good Example:
```
d = {'hello': 'world'}

print d.get('hello', 'default_value')   # prints 'world'
print d.get('thingy', 'default_value')  # prints 'default_value'

# Or:
if 'hello' in d:
    print d['hello']
```

Manipulate Lists the Short Way

You don't need to be long-winded when it comes to manipulating lists; use list comprehensions or the **filter()** or **map()** functions to use concise syntax when you want to perform an operation on a list.

A Bad Example:
```
# Filter all elements that are more than 4
a = [5, 4, 3]
b = []
```

```
for i in a:
    if i > 4:
        b.append(i)
```

A Good Example:
```
a = [5, 4, 3]
b = [i for i in a if i > 4]
# Or:
b = filter(lambda x: x > 4, a)
```

Another Bad Example:
```
# Add 3 to all members f the list.
a = [5, 4, 3]
for i in range(len(a)):
    a[i] += 3
```

Another Good Example:
```
a = [5, 4, 3]
a = [i + 3 for i in a]
# Or:
a = map(lambda i: i + 3, a)
```

You can also use the function **enumerate()** to keep an account of where you are in a list:

```
a = [5, 4, 3]
for i, item in enumerate(a):
    print i, item
# prints
# 0 5
# 1 4
# 2 3
```

This function reads better than trying to manually handle a counter and it is far more optimal for iterators

Reading from a File
When you want to read from a file, it is best to use the **with open** syntax as this will close the files for you automatically.

A Bad Example:
```
f = open('file.txt')
a = f.read()
print a
f.close()
```

A Good Example:
```
with open('file.txt') as f:
    for line in f:
        print line
```

Using the **with** statement is far more efficient because it makes sure the file is always closed even when the **with** block contains an exception

Line Continuations
There are accepted limits to logical code lines and when you have one that is longer, it should be split up over several lines. Your Python interpreter will take consecutive lines and, so long as the final character on each line is a backslash (/), it will join the lines. However, although this can be useful sometimes, really

you should avoid doing it because it can be fragile. If you were to add a whitespace after the backslash, it can break your code and the results might not be what you expected.

A better way to do this is to enclose elements inside parentheses. If there is an unclosed parenthesis at the end of the line, the next line will be joined, and so on until there is a closed parenthesis. You could also use square or curly braces to do the same thing, so long as you remain consistent – whatever you use to start, you must also use to finish.

A Bad Example:

```
an_incredibly_big_string = """For many years I would go to bed early. Sometimes, \
    after I had put out my light, my eyes would shut so fast that I would not even \
    have the time to say "I am going to sleep.""""

from some.module.inside.another.module import a_good_function, another_good_function, \
    yet_another_good_function
```

A Good Example:

```
my_incredibly_big_string = (
    "For many years, I would go to bed early. Sometimes, "
    "when I had put out my light, my eyes would shut so fast "
```

```
    "that I would not even have time to
say "I am going to sleep.""
)

from     some.module.inside.another.module
import (
    a_good_function,
another_good_function,
yet_another_good_function)
```

That said, if you find that you are having to keep on splitting up long lines, it is just a sign that you are trying to do too much and this will affect the readability of the code

Chapter 7: Method and Function Arguments

For the first argument in any instance method always use self and, for the first argument in any class method, always use cls.

If the name of a function's argument is the same as one of the reserved keywords, then it is best to add one trailing underscore than it is to use a corrupted spelling or an abbreviation. As such, you should `class_` rather than `clss`. Perhaps even better than causing a clash - use a synonym.

Function Arguments

There are 4 ways that you can pass an argument to a function:

1. **Positional Argument** – these are mandatory and do not contain any default values. The positional is the simplest argument form and are used for the arguments that are a complete part of the meaning of a function; they also have a natural order so, in the following example, the function user should find it easy to remember that the 2 functions need 2 arguments and they should remember the order:

`Send(message, recipient)` and `point(x, y)`

In both cases, you can use the argument names when you call the functions and, by doing this, you can change the order the arguments are in. For example, you could call `send(recipient='world', message='Hello')` and `point(y=2, x=1)`. However, as you can see from this, it is not very readable and there are way more words there than we need. Compare that version to the one that is more straightforward – `send('Hello', 'World')` and `point(1,2)` and you can see the difference in readability instantly.

2. **Keyword Argument** – these do contain default values and they are not mandatory. Keyword arguments are sometimes used for optional parameters that you send to the function. When a function contains at least 2 or 3, preferably more, positional parameters, it is not easy to remember. Using a keyword argument that has a default value is more helpful. For example, you could define a complete **send** function as `send(message, to, cc=None, bcc=None)`. The use of `cc` and `bcc` is optional and both have a value of `None` if they are not given another value.

There are a few ways that you can call a function with a keyword argument in Python. For example, you could follow the argument order in a definition and no explicitly name those arguments; for example, `send('Hello',`

`'World'`, `'Galactus'`, `'God'`). In this, you are sending a carbon copy of the message to Galactus and a blind carbon copy to God. You can also name the arguments in a different order, for example, `send('Helloagain'`, `'World'`, `bcc='God'`, `cc='Galactus'`). Unless you have a very good reason not to follow the correct syntax as closely as possible, these two examples are best avoided; they are verbose and not readable. The best way, the way that is closest to the function definition, is `send('Hello'`, `'World'`, `cc='Galactus'`, `bcc='God'`).

3. **Arbitrary Argument List** - This is the next way of passing an argument to a function. Sometimes, the intention of a function is better expressed with a signature that has a number of positional arguments, a number that can be extended. In that case, you are better using the `*args` constructs to define it. In the body of the argument, `args` is a tuple of all of the positional arguments that are left. For example, you can use `send(message, *args)` and list all of the recipients as a separate argument: `send('Hello'`, `'Galactus'`, `'Dad'`, `'God'`) — in the body of the function, `*args` is equal to (`'Galactus'`, `'Dad'`, `'God'`)

However, you should really use this construct cautiously because it does have some drawbacks. If a function is sent a list that contains arguments that are of the same or similar nature, a better definition would be a function of a single argument; that single argument would be a sequence or a list. For example, if `send` had several recipients, you would be better with an explicit definition: `send('Hello', 'God', 'Dad', 'Galactus')` and then call it by using `send('Hello',['God', 'Dad', 'Galactus'])`. In this way, the function user can change the recipient list beforehand and that opens up the possibility for any sequence that can't be unpacked to be passed, and that includes iterators.

4. **Arbitrary Keyword Argument Dictionary** - This is final way of passing an argument to a function. If a function needs an unknown array of named arguments, you can use the construct `**kwargs`. Within the body of the function, ****kwargs** is a dictionary that contains all of the named arguments that have been passed and not caught by another keyword argument in the signature of the function

However, you should use the same level of caution that you did with arbitrary argument lists, for pretty much the same reasons. These are powerful techniques that should only be used when you can prove that it is necessary to use them. They most definitely should not be used if there is a clearer and simpler construct that will do the job.

It really is down to you, the programmer, to decide which of the function arguments are optional keywords and which are positional and to determine whether you should use the more advanced techniques to pass the arguments.

Keep it simple and follow these rules of writing Python functions that:

- Are readable – the names and the arguments do not need any explanations

- Are easily changeable – you can add a keyword argument in without the rest of the code breaking.

Chapter 8: Naming Conventions

To be honest, the Python library naming conventions are something of a mess so we are never going to be totally consistent. However, there are some naming standards that are recommended and all new packages and modules, and that includes any third-party frameworks, must be written to these standards. That said, if you are using an existing library with a different style, stick to that style because consistency is preferable, especially in terms of readability

The first and most important principle to learn is that, where you are using names that are a visible part of a public API, you must use a convention that reflects that usage of the name, rather than the implementation of it.

Descriptive

There are quite a few different naming styles so it is helpful to recognize which one is in use, independently of the usage. These are the most commonly distinguished naming styles:

- `B` – single uppercase
- `b` – single lowercase
- `lowercase_with_underscores`
- `lowercase`
- `UPPERCASE_WITH_UNDERSCORES`
- `UPPERCASE`
- `CapitalizedWords` – often called CamelCase because the letters look somewhat bumpy*

- `mixedCase` — different from CamelCase because the first letter is in lowercase
- `Capital_Words_With_Underscore` - not a pretty style!

* When you use abbreviations in CamelCase, you should make sure all of the abbreviation letters are capitalized. For example, rather than using `HttpServerError`, use `HTTPServerError` instead

You can also use another style, that of putting a unique prefix, a short one, that puts a group of related names together. This doesn't get used very much in Python but I mention it just so that you know it is there. An example would be the function `os.stat()` - this will return a tuple that contains items that have names like `st_size, st_mode, st_mtime` and so on.

These are some of the forms that use a trailing or a leading underscore and can usually be combined with any of the case conventions:

- `_one_leading_underscore` - this is generally an indicator of "internal use" that is not very strong.

- `One_trailing_underscore_` - generally used to stop a conflict with a Python keyword, for example:

```
Apinter.Toplevel(master,class_='Cla
ssName")
```

- `__two_leading_underscores` – when you name a class attribute, this invokes mangling of a name, for example: `(inside class FootBar, __boo)` would become `(_FootBar__boo)`

- `__two_leading_and_two_trailing_underscores` are attributes or "magic" objects that reside in a namespace that is user-controlled. For example: `__init__`, `__file__`, or `__import__`.

Prescriptive

These are the names you should avoid:

Never use 'O' (uppercase oh), 'l' (lowercase el) or 'I' (uppercase eye) when you are writing variable names of a single character. Depending on what font you are using, these may be, these can be confused with the numbers 'o' and '1' – if you do find yourself thinking about using 'l', use the uppercase 'L' instead.

Names for Modules and Packages

All module names should be short and lowercase. You can use an underscore in a module name but only if it makes it more readable. The same goes for Python packages –

short and lowercase names – but don't use underscores.

Where you have an extension module that has been written in C or in C++ and it is accompanied by a Python module that has an interface that is more object-oriented, the C or C++ module will have a leading underscore, for example, `_socket`

Class Names
Class names usually use the CapWords or CamelCase convention.

Built-in names have their own separate convention and are usually a single word or 2 words in one, for example, `'Hello'` or `'HelloWorld'`. The CamelCase convention tends to be kept for built-in constants and for exception names.

Type Variables
The names of the type variables usually use CamelCase and short names are preferred, for example, `Num`, `AnyStr`. You should add a suffix (_co or _contra) to the variables to declare contravariant or covariant behavior. For example:

```
Import TypeVar
```

Would become

```
VT_co = TypeVar('VT_co', covariant=True)
KT_contra = TypeVar('KT_contra',
contravariant=True)
```

Names of Exceptions

Exceptions are classes and, as such, you should use the class convention for naming. That said, if the exception is an error, make sure that you use the 'Error' suffix on the name.

Global Variables

Provided the variable is used inside a single module, the naming conventions are the same as for naming functions.

Functions

All function names are in lowercase and the words are separated by an underscore where needed to make it more readable. mixedCase conventions are only to be used in the context where this is already the style in order to keep backward compatibility intact.

Instance Variables and Method Names

Again, the naming conventions for functions apply here – using lowercase with intermittent underscores. If you are using an instance variable or a non-public method, you should use a single leading underscore. To stop a name from clashing with a subclass, two leading underscores should be used as a way of invoking the name mangling rules in Python.

When these rules are invoked, the name is mangled with the class name. For example, class Foo contains an attribute called `__a`. This cannot be accessed using `Foo.__a`. As a rule, you should only use a double leading underscore when the name is likely to come into conflict with class attributes that are designed as subclasses.

Constants

These tend to be defined on module level and are all uppercase with separating underscores, for example, `MAX_OVERFLOW`

Inheritance Design

One rule to abide by is to determine if the instance variable or class method is non-public or public. If you can't decide, go for non-public as you can easily change it to public later on, whereas changing public to non-public is not so easy.

A public attribute is one that clients that are not related to the class would use while a non-public attribute is one that is not intended for use by a third-party. With a public attribute, you guarantee backward compatibility from start to finish while, with the non-pubic attribute you do not and can remove or make changes to the attribute. Note that the term "private" is not used and this is because there is no real private attribute in the Python language.

One other attribute category is that which is a protected attribute. In Python, they come under the subclass API. There are those classes that are designed solely as classes to inherit from, whether it is as a way of extending or modifying certain aspects of the behavior. When you design a class like this, always make sure that you make explicit decisions about the attributes – are they public, only to be used by the base class or are they in the subclass API?

With all of this, these are the Pythonic guidelines:

- A public attribute must not have a leading underscore

- If a public attribute clashes with a keyword (reserved), add one trailing underscore to the attribute name. This is the preferred method over using a corruption in spelling or an abbreviation.

- With a public data attribute, the best way is to expose only the name of the attribute, without using any complicated mutator or accessor methods. If a simple attribute needs to expand its functional behavior, Python makes it easy.

- If you are using a class that is going to be subclassed and you are also using attributes that are not going to be subclassed, think about adding 2 leading underscores but do not add in any trailing underscores. This will invoke name mangling and helps to lower the risk of name clashes if the subclasses have attributes with the same name in them.

Chapter 9: Using Whitespace in Statements and Expressions

First, some of the peeves about whitespaces:

Do not use unnecessary whitespaces in these cases:

- Immediately within braces, brackets or parentheses

A Good Example:
```
ham(spam[1], {eggs: 2})
```

A Bad Example:
```
ham( spam[ 1 ], { eggs: 2 } )
```

- Immediately in front of a colon, semicolon or a comma:

A Good Example:
```
if x == 4: print x, y; x, y = y, x
```

A Bad Example:
```
if x == 4 : print x , y ; x , y = y , x
```

However, where you have a slice, the colon is similar to a binary operator and it should contain an equal amount on each side. Where you have an extended slice, both of the colons must contain the exact same level of spacing. The exception to this is a slice parameter that has been omitted, along with the space.

A Good Example:
```
spam[1:8], spam[1:8:2], spam[:8:2],
spam[1::2], spam[1:8:]
```

```
spam[lower:upper], spam[lower:upper:],
spam[lower::step]
spam[lower+offset : upper+offset]
spam[: upper_fn(x) : step_fn(x)], ham[::
step_fn(x)]
spam[lower + offset : upper + offset]
```

A Bad Example:
```
spam[lower + offset:upper + offset]
spam[1: 8], ham[1 :8], ham[1:8 :2]
spam[lower : : upper]
spam[ : upper]
```

- Right before the opening parenthesis that begins the argument list of the function call:

A Good Example:
```
ham(1)
```

A Bad Example:
```
ham (1)
```

- Right in front of the open parenthesis that starts a slicing or an indexing:

A Good Example:
```
dct['key'] = lst[index]
```

A Bad Example:
```
dct ['key'] = lst [index]
```

- When there is more than a single space around an operator, such as an assignment, that aligns it with another operator

A Good Example:
```
x = 1
y = 2
long_variable = 3
```

A Bad Example:
```
x             = 1
y             = 2
long_variable = 3
```

Other Recommendations

Avoid having trailing whitespace throughout your code because it is not visible and it can cause confusion. For example, if you put in a backslash and follow it with a space and then a newline – this would not be counted as a line continuation. In fact, some text editors will not preserve it and there are projects that contain pre-commit hooks that will simply reject it – one of those is CPython.

The following binary operators should be surrounded by single spaces – one on each side:

- assignment (=)
- augmented assignment (+=, = etc.)

The following comparisons are treated the same:

- ==

- <
- >
- !=
- <>
- <=
- >=
- in
- not in
- is
- is not

And these Booleans:

- and
- or
- not

If you use operators that have different priorities, think about putting whitespace around the lowest priority operators – use your best judgment here. However, you should not use any more than a single space and make sure that each side of the operator has the same amount of whitespace – don't put 1 on one side and 2 on the other:

A Good Example:
```
i = i + 1
submitted += 1
x = x*2 - 1
hypot2 = x*x + y*y
c = (a+b) * (a-b)
```

A Bad Example:
```
i=i+1
submitted +=1
x = x * 2 - 1
hypot2 = x * x + y * y
c = (a + b) * (a - b)
```

When you use an = sign to indicate default values for parameters or keyword arguments, do not use whitespace around the sign:

A Good Example:
```
def complex(real, imag=0.0):
    return magic(r=real, i=imag)
```

A Bad Example:
```
def complex(real, imag = 0.0):
    return magic(r = real, i = imag)
```

Use the standard rules for colons with function annotations and make sure there are spaces surrounding the -> if it is used:

A Good Example:
```
def munge(input: AnyStr): ...
def munge() -> AnyStr: ...
```

A Bad Example:
```
def munge(input:AnyStr): ...
def munge()->PosInt: ...
```

When you combine a default value and an argument annotation, spaces should surround the = sign – do not do this unless the argument has both the default and the annotation:

A Good Example:
```
def munge(sep: AnyStr = None): ...
def munge(input: AnyStr, sep: AnyStr = None, limit=1000): ...
```

A Bad Example:
```
def munge(input: AnyStr=None): ...
def munge(input: AnyStr, limit = 1000):
...
```

It is not good practice to use compound statements – several statements on one line:

A Good Example:
```
if foo == 'that':
    do_that_thing()
do_one()
do_two()
do_three()
```

Best Not to Do:
```
if foo == 'that': do_that_thing()
do_one(); do_two(); do_three()
```

It is, on occasion, alright to use an if, for and while statement on one line, provided they have small bodies but you should never do this for statements that have several clauses. Also, never fold really long lines:

Best Not to Do:
```
if foo == 'that': do_that_thing()
for x in lst: total += x
while t < 10: t = delay()
```

Most Definitely Not:
```
if foo == 'that': do_that_thing()
else: do_non_that_thing()

try: something()
finally: cleanup()

do_one();    do_two();     do_three(long, argument,
                                list,   like, this)

if foo == 'that': one(); two(); three()
```

Conclusion

Thank you once again for reading my book, I truly hope that it was able to help you understand how to write more effective and efficient Python code.

From here, the next step is to, quite simply, practice. The more you do, the better you will get and, eventually, you will be writing Python code like a pro! Research, join online Python forums and join the Python community to learn more and to advance your skills.

Lastly, if you found this book helpful, please can I ask a small favor of you? Please consider leaving a review for me at Amamzon.com; it isn't only helpful to me, it also benefits prospective readers

Thank you and good luck on your journey to becoming a better Python programmer

Python:

Advanced Guide to Programming Code with Python

Charlie Masterson

Introduction

I want to thank you and congratulate you for downloading the book, *"Python: Advanced Guide to Programming Code with Python"*.

This book contains advanced steps and strategies on how to further your Python programming knowledge.

This book is exactly what the title says – advanced so, if you have little to no knowledge of programming with Python, this really isn't the book for you. It is aimed at those who are competent at basic Python programming and want to further their knowledge by learning some of the more advanced concepts but this is by no means a comprehensive guide to all the advanced programming concepts. Instead I have picked some of the more important ones that you should learn and I hope that you gain something from reading this and working through the code examples.

Thanks again for downloading this book, I hope you enjoy it!

Chapter 1: Python Comprehensions

Once you get to know a list comprehension, once you get what they are, you will find that they become quite compelling. So, what is a Python comprehension? Basically, they are constructs that let a sequence be built from another sequence. Python 2.0 introduced list comprehensions while Python 3.0 continues with set and dictionary comprehensions.

List Comprehensions

A list comprehension is made up of the following components:

- Input sequence
- Variable that represents the members of that input sequence
- Optional predicate expression
- Output expression – this satisfies the predicate by taking the input sequence members and producing the elements of the output list

Let's say that you want a list of the integers that are in a sequence and then you want to square them:

Example codes:

```
a_list = [1, '4', 9, 'a', 0, 4]
```

```
squared_ints = [ e**2 for e in a_list if
type(e) == types.IntType ]

print squared_ints
# [ 1, 81, 0, 16 ]
```

Here's how that works:

- The iterator part of the statement will iterate through each individual member if the input sequence known as a_list
- The predicate will then check to see if each one is an integer
- If it is, it will be passed to the output expression and then squared, becoming a member in the output list

You can get pretty much the same result if you use the Python built-in functions, filter and map or the lambda function:

The map function will modify the members in the sequence:

```
map(lambda e: e**2, a_list)
```

While the filter function will apply a predicate to the sequence:

```
filter(lambda       e:      type(e)      ==
types.IntType, a_list)
```

You can combine these:

```
map(lambda    e:    e**2,    filter(lambda    e:
type(e) == types.IntType, a_list))
```

Ok, so this example is showing you three function calls – *map*, *type* and *filter* – and two calls to *lambda*. Just be aware that Python function calls can be expensive and note that the input sequence has been traversed twice and filter is what produces an intermediate list.

List comprehensions are enclosed in lists so it is very easy to see that a list has been produced. You don't need any call to lambda and only one to type; instead, list comprehensions use iterators, which we will talk about more in the next chapter, as well as an expression and, if you use the optional predicate, an if expression.

Nested Comprehensions

Take an identity matrix, size n. That is a square matrix of n by n and the ones will be listed on the main diagonal.

A 3 by 3 example of that is:

1	0	0
0	1	0
0	0	1

In Python, we would represent this matrix by using a list of lists. Each of the sub-lists is representative of a row and a 3 by 3 matrix would be shown by way of this code:

```
[ [ 1, 0, 0 ],
  [ 0, 1, 0 ],
  [ 0, 0, 1 ] ]
```

To generate this matrix, we would use this comprehension:

```
[ [ 1 if item_idx == row_idx else 0 for item_idx in range(0, 3) ] for row_idx in range(0, 3) ]
```

Techniques

By using zip() you can deal with at least two elements at any one time:

```
['%s=%s' % (n, v) for n, v in zip(self.all_names, self)]
```

To automatically unpack a tuple, you can use multiple types:

```
[f(v) for (n, f), v in zip(cls.all_slots, values)]
```

You can use `os.walk()` for a two-level list comprehension:

```
# Comprehensions/os_walk_comprehension.py
import os
```

```
restFiles = [os.path.join(d[0], f) for d
in os.walk(".")
            for   f    in    d[2]     if
f.endswith(".rst")]
for r in restFiles:
    print(r)
```

A more complicated example of that will give you a description of all of the parts:

```
# CodeManager.py
"""
TODO: Break the check into two pieces?
TODO: update() this is still in test
mode; it doesn't actually work properly
yet.
```

Another way of doing this would be to place the codeMarker and the first line (which should be indented) into the restructures text file and then you can run the update program, which will insert the rest automatically:

```
CODE:

"""
import os, re, sys, shutil, inspect,
difflib

restFiles = [os.path.join(d[0], f) for d
in os.walk(".") if not "_test" in d[0]
            for   f    in    d[2]     if
f.endswith(".rst")]
Classes
class Python:
        codeMarker = "::\n\n"
```

```
        commentTag = "#"
        listings   =   re.compile("::\n\n(
{4}#.*(?:\n+ {4}.*)*)")
class Java:
        codeMarker =  "..   code-block::
java\n\n"
        commentTag = "//"
        listings = \
          re.compile("..    *code-block::
*java\n\n( {4}//.*(?:\n+ {4}.*)*)")
```

def shift(name of listing):

```
    "this will move the listing to the
left by 4 spaces"
    return [x[4:] if x.startswith("    ")
else x for x in listing.splitlines()]

# TEST - this makes duplicates of all the
.rst files that are in a test directory
to test update():
dirs    =    set([os.path.join("_test",
os.path.dirname(f)) for f in restFiles])
if [os.makedirs(d) for d in dirs if not
os.path.exists(d)]:
    [shutil.copy(f, os.path.join("_test",
f)) for f in restFiles]
testFiles = [os.path.join(d[0], f) for d
in os.walk("_test")
         for   f   in   d[2]    if
f.endswith(".rst")]
```

class Commands:

```
    """
Each of the static methods is able to be
called from the command line so you would
```

```
add in a new static method at this point
to add a new command into the program
    """

    @staticmethod
    def display(language):
        """
        Print all of the code listings
that are in the .rst files.
        """
        for f in restFiles:
            listings = language.listings.findall(open(f).read())
            if not listings: continue
            print('=' * 60 + "\n" + f + "\n" + '=' * 60)
            for n, l in enumerate(listings):
                print("\n".join(shift(l)))
                if n < len(listings) - 1:
                    print('-' * 60)

    @staticmethod
```

def extract(name of language):

```
        """
Pull all of the code listings from the
.rst files and then write each one into
its own file. This will not overwrite in
the event that the .rst files and the
code files do not agree unless you insert
"extract -force"
        """
        force = len(sys.argv) == 3 and sys.argv[2] == '-force'
        paths = set()
```

```python
        for listing in [shift(listing)
for f in restFiles
            for listing in
language.listings.findall(open(f).read())
]:
        path =
listing[0][len(language.commentTag):].strip()
        if path in paths:
            print("ERROR: Duplicate file name: %s" % path)
            sys.exit(1)
        else:
            paths.add(path)
        path = os.path.join("..", "code", path)
        dirname = os.path.dirname(path)
        if dirname and not os.path.exists(dirname):
            os.makedirs(dirname)
        if os.path.exists(path) and not force:
            for i in difflib.ndiff(open(path).read().splitlines(), listing):
                if i.startswith("+ ") or i.startswith("- "):
                    print("ERROR: Existing file different from .rst")
                    print("Use 'extract -force' to force overwrite")

Commands.check(language)
        return
    file(path, 'w').write("\n".join(listing))
```

```
@staticmethod
def check(name of language):
    """
    Make sure that all the external
    code files exist and then check which of
    the external files have changed the
    contents of the .rst files. This
    generates files in the subdirectory
    called _deltas to show what changes have
    been made
    """
    class Result: # Messenger
        def __init__(self, **kwargs):
            self.__dict__ = kwargs
    result = Result(missing = [], deltas = [])
    listings = [Result(code = shift(code), file = f)
                for f in restFiles
                for code in language.listings.findall(open(f).read())
                ]
    paths = [os.path.normpath(os.path.join("..", "code", path)) for path in
             [listing.code[0].strip()[len(language.commentTag):].strip()
              for listing in listings]]
    if os.path.exists("_deltas"):
        shutil.rmtree("_deltas")
    for path, listing in zip(paths, listings):
        if not os.path.exists(path):
```

```
result.missing.append(path)
            else:
                code = open(path).read().splitlines()
                for i in difflib.ndiff(listing.code, code):
                    if i.startswith("+ ") or i.startswith("- "):
                        d = difflib.HtmlDiff()
                        if not os.path.exists("_deltas"):
                            os.makedirs("_deltas")
                        html = os.path.join("_deltas", os.path.basename(path).split('.')[0] + ".html")
                        open(html, 'w').write(
                            "<html><h1>Left: %s<br>Right: %s</h1>" % (listing.file, path) +
                            d.make_file(listing.code, code))
                        result.deltas.append(Result(file = listing.file,
                                                    path = path, html = html, code = code))
                        break
        if result.missing:
            print("Missing %s files:\n%s" %
```

```
                    (language.__name__,
"\n".join(result.missing)))
            for delta in result.deltas:
                print("%s changed in %s; see %s" %
                    (delta.file, delta.path, delta.html))
            return result

    @staticmethod
```

def update(name of language): # *Test until this is deemed trustworthy*

```
        """
        Refresh the external code files into .rst files.
        """
        check_result = Commands.check(language)
        if check_result.missing:
            print(language.__name__, "update aborted")
            return
        changed = False
        def _update(matchobj):
            listing = shift(matchobj.group(1))
            path = listing[0].strip()[len(language.commentTag):].strip()
            filename = os.path.basename(path).split('.')[0]
            path = os.path.join("..", "code", path)
            code = open(path).read().splitlines()
```

```
        return language.codeMarker + \
            "\n".join([("    " + line).rstrip() for line in listing])
        for f in testFiles:
            updated = language.listings.sub(_update, open(f).read())
            open(f, 'w').write(updated)

if __name__ == "__main__":
    commands = dict(inspect.getmembers(Commands, inspect.isfunction))
    if len(sys.argv) < 2 or sys.argv[1] not in commands:
        print("Command line options:\n")
        for name in commands:
            print(name + ":  " + commands[name].__doc__)
    else:
        for language in inspect.getmembers(Languages, inspect.isclass):
            commands[sys.argv[1]](language[1])
```

Set Comprehensions

A set comprehension helps you to construct sets with the exact same principles as the list comprehension with just one difference – the result is a set, not a list. Let's say that you have a list of names; this list can contain those names that are different from the case that is used to represent them, which are duplicates and those that contain just one character. The names that we want are those that are longer than a single character and we want to represent all of the names in the same format. For this, all the first letters have to be capitalized while all other letters are lower case.

This is the list that you begin with:

```
names = [ 'Billy', 'JASON', 'alison', 'billy', 'ALISON', 'J', 'Billy' ]
The set that we want is:
{ 'Billy', 'Jason', 'Alison' }
```

Did you spot the new syntax used to denote a set? We enclose the members of the set inside curly braces {} and the following example shows you a set comprehension that does this:

```
{ name[0].upper() + name[1:].lower() for name in names if len(name) > 1 }
```

Dictionary Comprehensions

Let's say that you have a dictionary and the keys in it are characters. The values of those characters' map to how often the character appears in the text and the dictionary are able to determine the difference between lower and upper case characters.

What we want is a dictionary that combines the occurrences of lower and upper case characters and this is how you do it:

CODE:

```
mcase = {'a':10, 'b': 34, 'A': 7, 'Z':3}

mcase_frequency = { k.lower() : mcase.get(k.lower(), 0) + mcase.get(k.upper(), 0) for k in mcase.keys() }

# mcase_frequency == {'a': 17, 'z': 3, 'b': 34}
```

Chapter 2: Python Iterators

Iterators

Let's begin with iterators. In Python, iterator objects follow the iterator protocol while supporting two different methods. This is a requirement of Python:

- `__iter__` will return the iterator object. We use this in both the *in* and *for* statements
- `__next__` method will return the next value that comes from the iterator. If there are no more values to return, a `StopIteration` exception should be raised.

class Counter(name of object):

```
    def __init__(self, low, high):
        self.current = low
        self.high = high

    def __iter__(self):
        'Will return itself as an iterator object'
        return self

    def __next__(self):
        'will return the next value from the iterator until the current value is lower than high'
        if self.current > self.high:
            raise StopIteration
        else:
```

```
        self.current += 1
        return self.current - 1
```

This iterator can now be used in the code:

```
>>> c = Counter(1,5)
>>> for i in c:
...     print(i, end=' ')
...
1 2 3 4 5
```

Don't forget; we can only use an iterator object one single time and that means that, once `StopIteration` has been raised once, the same exception will keep on being raised

```
>>> c = Counter(2,3)
>>> next(c)
2
>>> next(c)
3
>>> next(c)
Traceback (the most recent call last):
File "<stdin>", line 1, in <module>
File "<stdin>", line 11, in next
StopIteration
>>> next(c)
Traceback (the most recent call last):
File "<stdin>", line 1, in <module>
File "<stdin>", line 11, in next
StopIteration
```

If you use the iterator in the `for` loop, the next example will try to show what the code is behind the scenes:

```
>>> iterator = iter(c)
>>> while True:
...     try:
...         x = iterator.__next__()
...         print(x, end=' ')
...     except StopIteration as e:
...         break
...
1 2 3 4 5
```

Chapter 3: Python Generators

Now we look at Python generators, first introduced with Python v2.3. Generators are a much easier way of creating iterators from a function by using the keyword *yield:*

```
>>> def my_generator():
...     print("Inside my generator")
...     yield 'a'
...     yield 'b'
...     yield 'c'
...
>>> my_generator()
<generator object my_generator at 0x7fbcfa0a6aa0>
```

So, in this example, we created a very simple generator by using the `yield` statements and, like any other iterator, you can use it in a `for` loop:

```
>>> for char in my_generator():
...     print(char)
...
Inside the generator
a
b
c
```

Here is another example where we create the `Counter` class through the use of a generator function and then we use it inside a `for` loop:

```
def counter_generator(low, high):
    while low <= high:
        yield low
        low += 1
```

```
>>> for i in counter_generator(1,5):
...     print(i, end=' ')
...
1 2 3 4 5
```

When the `while` loop gets to the `yield` statement, inside the loop you will notice that the return is a value of low and generator state becomes suspended. Now look at the second `next` call; the generator has resumed from where it stopped before and the value is increased by one. The `while` loop will continue round to the `yield` statement.

When you call generator functions, they return *generator* objects so, if you were to call *dir* on the object you would find that it has the *__next__* and the __iter__ methods included, along with some other methods:

```
>>> c = counter_generator(1,5)
>>> dir(c)
['__class__',            '__delattr__',
'__dir__',      '__doc__',      '__eq__',
'__format__',
'__ge__',  '__getattribute__',  '__gt__',
'__hash__', '__init__', '__iter__',
'__le__', '__lt__', '__name__', '__ne__',
'__new__', '__next__', '__reduce__',
'__reduce_ex__',             '__repr__',
'__setattr__',  '__sizeof__',   '__str__',
'__subclasshook__',
'close',        'gi_code',      'gi_frame',
'gi_running', 'send', 'throw']
```

We tend to use generators as a way of making lazy evaluations and, in this way, they become one of the best approaches when you are working with a lot of data. If you don't want to go down the route of loading all of your data into memory, a generator can be used to pass you the data one piece at a time.

Perhaps the biggest and best example of this is the function `os.path.walk()`. This will use a callback function together with the `os.walk` generator. Using this generator will save a ton of memory. There are generators which can produce infinite values and this is an example of one:

```
>>> def infinite_generator(start=0):
...     while True:
...         yield start
...         start += 1
...
>>> for num in infinite_generator(1):
...     print(num, end=' ')
...     if num > 15:
...         break
...
1 2 3 4 5 6 7 8 9 10 11 12 13 14 15 16
```

If we were to go back to the `my_generator` example you would find out one thing about generators – they cannot be re-used. Remember, we said they are single use only:

```
>>> g = my_generator()
>>> for c in g:
...     print(c)
...
Inside my_generator you would see
a
```

```
b
c
>>> for c in g:
...     print(c)
...
```

There is a way to create a generator that can be reused and that is to use a generator that is Object-based because these do not hold a state. Any class that contains an __iter__ method that yields data may be used as an object generator and, in the following example, we will create the Counter generator:

```
>>> class Counter(object):
...     def __init__(self, low, high):
...         self.low = low
...         self.high = high
...     def __iter__(self):
...         counter = self.low
...         while self.high >= counter:
...             yield counter
...             counter += 1
...
>>> gobj = Counter(1, 5)
>>> for num in gobj:
...     print(num, end=' ')
...
1 2 3 4 5
>>> for num in gobj:
...     print(num, end=' ')
...
1 2 3 4 5
```

Generator Expressions

Generator expressions are a way of generalizing generators and list comprehensions in a memory-efficient and high-performance way. In this next example, we are going to try summing up the squares of all numbers between 1 and 9:

```
>>> sum([x*x for x in range(1,10)])
```

What we have done here is create a list that contains the square values in memory. We then iterate over the list and, after the sum, the memory is freed. This is better understood where you have a bigger list. The generator expression can be used to save memory:

```
sum(x*x for x in range(1,10))
```

The syntax that we use for the generator expression dictates that it must always be directly within parentheses and must not contain a comma either side of it. This means that either of the examples below can be used as valid generator expressions:

```
>>> sum(x*x for x in range(1,10))
285
>>> g = (x*x for x in range(1,10))
>>> g
<generator object <genexpr> at 0x7fc559516b90>
```

You can chain generators or generator expressions and, with the following example, we are going to read a file called */var/log/cron*. We are looking to see if there are any specific jobs that are running successfully or not – we are looking for one called anacron. You can also achieve the same with the shell command `tail -f /var/log/cron |grep anacron`

```
>>> jobtext = 'anacron'
>>> all = (line for line in open('/var/log/cron', 'r') )
>>> job = ( line for line in all if line.find(jobtext) != -1)
>>> text = next(job)
>>> text
"May    6   12:17:15   dhcp193-104 anacron[23052]:   Job   `cron.daily' terminated\n"
>>> text = next(job)
>>> text
'May    6   12:17:15   dhcp193-104 anacron[23052]:  Normal  exit  (1  job run)\n'
>>> text = next(job)
>>> text
'May    6   13:01:01   dhcp193-104   run-parts(/etc/cron.hourly)[25907]:  starting 0anacron\n
```

Chapter 4: Python Decorators

Decorators give us a way of calling higher-order functions by using a much simpler syntax. The definition of a Python decorator is "a function that takes another function and then extends the behavior of the last function without explicit modification". That probably sounds incredibly confusing but, really, it isn't and you will see that through the following examples:

Example 1:

```
def my_decorator(some_function):

    def wrapper():

        print("Something happens before we call some_function()")

        some_function()

        print("Something happens after we call some_function()")

    return wrapper


def just_some_function():
    print("Whee!")


just_some_function = my_decorator(just_some_function)

just_some_function()
```

Have a guess at what the output of this code is going to be. I'll give you a couple of clues – something happens before we call `some_function` and then something happens after we call `some_function`

Simply put, a decorator wraps a function and modifies the behavior of the function. Let's add in an *if* statement:

Example 2:

```
def my_decorator(some_function):

    def wrapper():

        num = 10

        if num == 10:
            print("Yes!")
        else:
            print("No!")

        some_function()

        print("Something happens after we call some_function()")

    return wrapper


def just_some_function():
    print("Whee!")
```

```
just_some_function                    =
my_decorator(just_some_function)

just_some_function()
```

The result of this is the output:

```
Yes!
Whee!
Something   happens    after   we    call
some_function().
```

Python lets you use the "pie" syntax (the @ symbol) to make calling a decorator much simpler.

Next, we are going to create a module for the decorator:

```
def my_decorator(some_function):

    def wrapper():

        num = 10

        if num == 10:
            print("Yes!")
        else:
            print("No!")

        some_function()

        print("Something happens after we call some_function() .")

    return wrapper
```

```
if __name__ == "__main__":
    my_decorator()
```

Okay, still with me? Hang on there because all will become clear. Now we are going to call the function using the decorator:

```
from decorator07 import my_decorator

@my_decorator
def just_some_function():
    print("Whee!")

just_some_function()
```

When this example is run, the output should be exactly the same as the last one:

```
Yes!
Whee!
Something happens after we call some_function().
```

So, using `@my_decorator` is a much better and easier way of saying `just_some_function = my_decorator(just_some_function)` and this is the way that a decorator is applied to a function.

Let's look at a few real-world examples:

CODE:

```python
import time

def timing_function(some_function):

    """
    Will outputs the time that a function takes
    to execute.
    """

    def wrapper():
        t1 = time.time()
        some_function()
        t2 = time.time()
        return "Time it took to run the function: " + str((t2 - t1)) + "\n"
    return wrapper


@timing_function
def my_function():
    num_list = []
    for num in (range(0, 10000)):
        num_list.append(num)
    print("\nSum of all the numbers: " + str((sum(num_list))))


print(my_function())
```

The output will be the time before `my_function()` was run and the time after it. The next step is to subtract one number from the other to get the time taken to run the function

Have a good look at it; run the code and work through it, one line at a time and ensure that you fully understand how it all works:

```python
from time import sleep


def sleep_decorator(function):

    """
    This limits how fast the function may be
    called.
    """

    def wrapper(*args, **kwargs):
        sleep(2)
        return function(*args, **kwargs)
    return wrapper


@sleep_decorator
def print_number(num):
    return num

print(print_number(222))

for num in range(1, 6):
    print(print_number(num))
```

We use this decorator for rate limiting – test it out and see what happens.

One of the most popular of all the Python decorators is `login_required()`. This makes sure that a person is logged in or authenticated properly before a specific route can be accessed, in this case `/secret`:

```
from functools import wraps
from flask import g, request, redirect, url_for


def login_required(f):
    @wraps(f)
    def decorated_function(*args, **kwargs):
        if g.user is None:
            return redirect(url_for('login', next=request.url))
        return f(*args, **kwargs)
    return decorated_function


@app.route('/secret')
@login_required
def secret():
    pass
```

What did you notice about this? Did you spot that the function has been passed back to the decorator `functools.wraps()`?

One last example: this is a Flask route handler:

```
@app.route('/grade', methods=['POST'])
def update_grade():
    json_data = request.get_json()
    if 'student_id' not in json_data:
        abort(400)
```

```
    # update database
    return "success!"
```

Here, we are making sure that the key called `student_id` is made a part of the request. While this does work, the validation really doesn't belong in the function. As well as that, there are other routes that may use the same validations so we use a decorator to take out any logic that is unnecessary:

```
from flask import Flask, request, abort
from functools import wraps

app = Flask(__name__)


def validate_json(*expected_args):
    def decorator(func):
        @wraps(func)
        def wrapper(*args, **kwargs):
            json_object = request.get_json()
            for expected_arg in expected_args:
                if expected_arg not in json_object:
                    abort(400)
            return func(*args, **kwargs)
        return wrapper
    return decorator

@app.route('/grade', methods=['POST'])
@validate_json('student_id')
def update_grade():
    json_data = request.get_json()
```

```
    print(json_data)
    # update database
    return "success!"
```

In this code, the decorator has taken a variable length list and used it as an argument and that lets us pass in whatever string arguments are necessary, as many as it takes. Each one will represent a key that is used in validating the JSON data.

One last thing before we leave this chapter – notice anything about that? New decorators are dynamically created based on the strings.

Chapter 5: Python Context Managers

Next to decorators, the Python Context Managers are the most common of all the constructs. And, like the decorators they are one of the things that you will use but probably won't truly understand how they work. As any school child will tell you, the easiest way to open a file and read from it is:

```
with open('what_are_context_managers.txt', 'r') as infile:
    for line in infile:
        print('> {}'.format(line))
```

The thing is, how many of you who handle file input and output (IO) properly know why it is the right way to handle it? Do you even now that there is a wrong way? Hopefully most of you otherwise this will all be a waste of time! But what do we use a context manager for?

Resource Management

Probably the most important, and the most common, use of a context manager is to manage resources properly. In fact, there is a good reason why a context manager is used when we read from a file. When we open a file, the very act of doing so uses a resource known as a file descriptor and your operating system limits this resource. By that, I mean that a process can only open up to a specific number of files at any one time. To prove the point, have a go at running this piece of code:

```
files = []
for x in range(100000):
    files.append(open('foo.txt', 'w'))
```

If you use a Linux or Mac OS computer, you will most likely see an error message that is similar to this one:

```
> python test.py
Traceback (the most recent call last):
  File "test.py", line 3, in <module>
OSError: [Errno 24] Too many open files: 'foo.txt'
```

If you are using Windows it might not be a good idea to try this; if you do, your computer will likely crash and your motherboard burst into flames! The lesson here is, do not leak a file descriptor!

All joking to one side (that won't really happen to your computer), the next question you should be asking is, "What is a file descriptor"? and then you should be asking what it means to "leak" a file descriptor. Let me try to explain – when a file is opened, the operating system will assign an integer to it and this lets it give you access to the file, instead, following direct access to the underlying file. This is good for several reasons, one of which being that you can pass references to the files between the processes. You can also maintain a certain security level that will be enforced by the kernel.

So, how do you "leak" one of these file descriptors? It's simple; when you open a file, you should always close it. If you don't, the file descriptor will leak. It is very easy to forget that you have files open, especially if you are working with several at once but, if you forget to close one, you will soon learn that there is normally a limit to how many file descriptors can be assigned to a process.

On a UNIX system or similar, typing `$ ulimit -n` at the command prompt should tell you what the value of the top limit is, but if you want to see more proof, run the example code above again but replace the number 100000 with whatever number came up when you ran `$ ulimit -n` less about 5, which will account for the files that are opened on startup by the Python interpreter. The code should now run through to completing.

Naturally, as always with Python, there is a much better and simpler way to make your program compete – make sure you close all of your open files. Here is a somewhat elaborate example of how you can fix the issue:

```
files = []
for x in range(10000):
    f = open('foo.txt', 'w')
    f.close()
    files.append(f)
```

An Even Better Way to Manage Your Resources

Of course, in a real system, it isn't all that easy to ensure that you call `close()` of every file that you open, especially if said file is inside a function that could cause an exception or that has a number of return paths. In a more complicated function that can open a file, how could you be expected to remember that you have to add `close()` to all of the places that a function can be returned from? And that is not including all of the exceptions which can come from anywhere. In short, you can't remember and neither can you be expected to.

In other computer programming languages, developers are forced into using `try...except...finally` every single time they work with files or any resource that has to be closed. Luckily, with Python, things are so much easier and we have a very simple way to ensure that all of the resources we have used are cleaned up properly, regardless of whether the code returns a result or if exceptions are thrown up – that solution is a context manager.

Things should be starting to look a little obvious by now. We need to find a convenient method that indicates a specific variable has a cleanup process associated with it. We also need to guarantee that, no matter what happens, the cleanup will happen. So, with that requirement in mind, the syntax that we use for a context manager actually makes a lot of sense:

```
with something_that_returns_a_context_manager(
) as my_resource:
    do_something(my_resource)
    ...
    print('done using my_resource')
```

That's all there is to it. Using `with`, you can call anything that can return a context manager, such as the `open()` function which is built in. You then assign that to a variable by using `...as<variable_name>`. The crucial thing to remember here is that the variable will only exist inside the indented block that is underneath the `with` statement.

It helps if you see the `with` statement as creating a kind of mini-function; the variable can be used freely inside the indented part but, as soon as that part finishes, the variable will go out of scope. When that happens, a special method is called containing the code that performs the cleanup.

But where, exactly, is that cleanup code? The short answer to that is, the code is wherever the context manager has been defined. There are several ways in which to create a context manager and the simplest way is to define a class containing two methods - __enter__() and __exit__(). The first method will return the resource that is to be managed, and the second method is the one that does the cleanup but doesn't return anything.

To make it all just a little bit clearer, we are going to create a context manager, that is completely redundant, that is for working with files:

```
class File():

    def __init__(self, filename, mode):
        self.filename = filename
        self.mode = mode

    def __enter__(self):
        self.open_file = open(self.filename, self.mode)
        return self.open_file

    def __exit__(self, *args):
        self.open_file.close()

files = []
for _ in range(10000):
    with File('foo.txt', 'w') as infile:
        infile.write('foo')
```

```
files.append(infile)
```

So, let's look at we have got here. Just like in any class, there is an `__init__()` method, responsible for setting up the object. In this case, we have set the file name to open and we have set the mode that it is to be opened up in. `__enter__()` opens the file and returns it, at the same time creating `attributeopen_file` — we can now refer to this in `__exit__()`.

`__exit__()` does nothing more than close the file. When you run the code above, it works because, when the file leaves the with file as `infile: block`, it closes the file. Even if the code within the block raised an exception, that file would still close.

Some More Useful Context Managers

Ok, so given that a context manager is very helpful, it is even more helpful that they have been put into the Standard Library in several different places. Some of the more useful ones are:

- `Lock objects in threading`
- `zipfile.Zipfiles`
- `subProcess.Popen`
- `tarfile.TarFile`
- `telnetib.Telner`
- `Pathlib.Path`

The list goes on forever. Basically, any object that you need to call close on after you have used it is a context manager, or at least, it should be.

One of the more interesting is Lock. In this case, the resource is a mutex and using a context manager stops common deadlock sources from happening in multi-threaded programs. These deadlocks happen when a thread manages to acquire a mutex and will not let go of it. Think about the following example:

from threading import Lock:

```
lock = Lock()

def do_something_dangerous():
    lock.acquire()
    raise Exception('oops I forgot this code could raise exceptions')
    lock.release()
```

try this:

```
    do_something_dangerous()
except:
    print('Got an exception')
lock.acquire()
print('Got here')
```

It is clear, or it should be that `lock.release()` won't be called and that will cause all of the other threads that call `do_something_dangerous()` to deadlock and, in this example, this is represented by not hitting the line that says `print('Got here')`. We can fix this very easily when we accept and take advantage of Lock being a context manager:

from threading import Lock:

```
lock = Lock()

def do_something_dangerous():
    with lock:
        raise Exception('oops I forgot, this code is able to raise exceptions')
```

try this:

```
    do_something_dangerous()
except:
    print('Got an exception')
lock.acquire()
print('Got here')
```

Really, there isn't any reasonable way of acquiring Lock through a context manager and then not releasing it and that is exactly as it should be.

Having Fun with `contextlib`

Because context managers are so very useful, there is an entire Standard Library module that is devoted to them and them alone. `contextlib` is full of useful tool for creating context managers and for working with them. One very good shortcut to create a context manager from classes is to use the decorator `@contextmanager`. You use this by decorating a generator function that will call yield only once. Anything that comes before the yield call is considered to be the code for `__enter__()` and everything after is the considered to be the code for `__exit__()`.

Let's rewrite the File context manager with the decorator:

from contextlib import contextmanager:

```
@contextmanager
def open_file(path, mode):
    the_file = open(path, mode)
    yield the_file
    the_file.close()

files = []

for x in range(100000):
    with open_file('foo.txt', 'w') as infile:
        files.append(infile)

for f in files:
    if not f.closed:
        print('not closed')
```

As you see, this is much shorter, only five lines. We have opened the file, we yielded it and then we closed it. The next set of code simply proves that the files have been closed and the other proof is the fact that your program did not crash.

There is a bit of a stupid but fun example that you can find in the official Python.docs but, for the sake of simplicity, here it is:

from contextlib import contextmanager:

```
@contextmanager
def tag(name):
    print("<%s>" % name)
    yield
    print("</%s>" % name)

>>> with tag("h1"):
...     print("foo")
...
<h1>
foo
</h1>
```

The best piece of stupidity and fun with context managers is `contextlib.ContextDecorator` because it allows you to use a class-based approach to defining a context manager while inheriting from `contextlib.ContextDecorator`. By doing this, you are able to use the context manager with the with statement as you would normally or as a function decorator. You could do something similar to the example above by using the following pattern – you shouldn't really do this though because it is just a little bit insane!

from contextlib import ContextDecorator:

```
class makeparagraph(ContextDecorator):
    def __enter__(self):
        print('<p>')
        return self

    def __exit__(self, *exc):
        print('</p>')
        return False

@makeparagraph()
def emit_html():
    print('Here is some non-HTML')

emit_html()
The output will be:
<p>
Here is some non-HTML
</p>
```

Totally useless and just a little horrifying!

Wrapping it Up

By now you should have some idea of what context managers are and how they work, not to mention why they are so useful. As you saw, there are quite a few things that you can do, some useful, some not so useful, with context managers. They have a noble goal in that they make it easier to work with your resources and it makes it much easier to manage created contexts. It's down to you to use these and to make new ones that make life easier for others – just don't make a habit of using them to generate HTML.

Chapter 6: Python Descriptors Overview

Descriptors were first introduced with Python v2.2 and they give us a way of adding a managed attribute to an object. We don't tend to use them in everyday computer programming but you do need to know all about them so that you understand quite a bit of the Python magic that goes on into the third-party packages and the standard library.

The Problem

Let's say that you own and run a bookshop. You use a Python-based inventory management system and that system has a class in it called Book. The class is used to capture the title, the author and the price of all your physical books:

```
class Book(object):
    def __init__(self, author, title, price):
        self.author = author
        self.title = title
        self.price = price

    def __str__(self):
        return "{0} - {1}".format(self.author, self.title)
```

Ok, so this simple class works well for a little while but, sooner or later bad data is going to get into the system. Your system will have loads of books that, because of errors in data entry, will have prices that are too high or even those that are negative. We decide that we want the prices of the books limited to somewhere between 0 and 100. Also, we have a class called Magazine and this has the exact same problem so the solution we come up with must be able to be reused easily.

The Descriptor Protocol

This protocol is nothing more than a set of methods that a class has to implement in order to be qualified as a descriptor. There are three methods:

- `__get__(self, instance, owner)`
- `__set__(self, instance, value)`
- `__delete__(self, instance)`

`__get__` is used to access values that are stored within the object and then return it
`__set__` is used to set a value that is stored within the object and will return nothing
`__delete__` is used to delete a value that is stored within the object and will return nothing

By using all three of these methods, we can create a descriptor that is named Price; this descriptor will place a limit on the stored values of between 0 and 100:

```
from weakref import WeakKeyDictionary
```

```
class Price(object):
    def __init__(self):
        self.default = 0
        self.values = WeakKeyDictionary()

    def __get__(self, instance, owner):
        return self.values.get(instance, self.default)

    def __set__(self, instance, value):
        if value < 0 or value > 100:
            raise ValueError("Price should be between 0 and 100.")
        self.values[instance] = value

    def __delete__(self, instance):
        del self.values[instance]
```

There are a few things that you need to be aware of in terms of the Price implementation:

- You must add an instance of any descriptor you use to the class and it must be a class attribute, not an instance attribute. That means, to store the data for each instance, the descriptor must maintain a dictionary and that dictionary must map instances to values that are instance-specific. In the Price implementation, the dictionary is named as `self.values`

- Python dictionaries will store references to the objects that are used as keys and those references, on their own, are sufficient to stop the object from being garbage collected. When we are finished with the Book instances, to stop them from hanging about we use `WeakKeyDictionary`, from `Weakref` standard module. As soon as the final strong reference passes on, the key pair associated with it will be discarded

Chapter 7: Using Python Descriptors

As you have seen, descriptors have a close link to classes and not to instances so, if you want to add a descriptor to the Book class, it has to be added as a class variable, not an instance:

```
class Book(object):
    price = Price()

    def __init__(self, author, title, price):
        self.author = author
        self.title = title
        self.price = price

    def __str__(self):
        return "{0} - {1}".format(self.author, self.title)
```

We have now enforced a Price constraint for the Books class

```
>>> b = Book("J K Rowling", "Harry Potter and the Chamber of Secrets", 12)
>>> b.price
12
>>> b.price = -12
Traceback (most recent call last):
  File "<pyshell#68>", line 1, in <module>
    b.price = -12
  File "<pyshell#58>", line 9, in __set__
    raise ValueError("Price should be between 0 and 100.")
ValueError: Price should be between 0 and 100.
>>> b.price = 101
```

```
Traceback (most recent call last):
  File "<pyshell#69>", line 1, in <module>
    b.price = 101
  File "<pyshell#58>", line 9, in __set__
    raise ValueError("Price should be between 0 and 100.")
ValueError: Price should be between 0 and 100.
```

How We Access Descriptors

Ok, so we have implemented a fully working descriptor, one that can manage the price attribute for the Book class but it may not be all that clear at this stage how it actually works. It all feels just a little bit like magic but it really isn't. In fact, accessing descriptors is really quite easy:

- When you attempt to evaluate `b.price` and get the value from it, Python will recognize Price as a descriptor and it will call `Book.price.__get__`
- When you attempt to change the price attribute value, for example, `b.price = 22`, Python will, once again, recognize price as a descriptor and will substitute the assignment with the call to `Book.price.__set__`
- And, lastly, when you attempt to delete a price attribute that is stored against a Book instance, Python will automatically

interpret it as the call to `Book.price.__delete__`

Unless you understand fully that a descriptor is linked to a class and not to an instance, and, as such, have to maintain mapping to instance-specific values, you could be very tempted to write your Price descriptor like this:

```
class Price(object):
    def __init__(self):
        self.__price = 0

    def __get__(self, instance, owner):
        return self.__price

    def __set__(self, instance, value):
        if value < 0 or value > 100:
            raise ValueError("Price should be between 0 and 100.")
        self.__price = value

    def __delete__(self, instance):
        del self.__price
```

However, once you begin to create multiple instance of Book, you are going to have a bit of a problem:

```
>>> b1 = Book("J K Rowling", "Harry Potter and the Chamber of Secrets", 12)
>>> b1.price

>>> b2 = Book("John Grisham", "Gray Mountain", 13)
>>> b1.price
```

They key is in understanding that there can only a single instance of Price for the Book class so, whenever the descriptor value is changed, it will change the value of all instances. That behavior is incredibly useful for when you want to create some managed class attributes but it isn't what we want for this. To store separate values that are instance-specific, you will need to use `WeakRefDictionary`.

Using the Property Built-In Function

There is another way to build a descriptor and that is with the property built-in function. This is the signature for the function:

```
property(fget=None,       fset=None,
fdel=None, doc=None)
```
- `fget` – a method to get an attribute
- `fset` – a method to set an attribute
- `fdel` – a method to delete an attribute
- `doc` is a docstring

So, rather than defining one class-level descriptor for the purpose of managing the instance-specific values, property built-in function works by joining the instance methods of the class. The following is a very simple example – we have a Publisher class from the Inventory system and it has a managed name property. Every method that is passed into Properly will have a print statement that shows when the method is called:

```
class Publisher(object):
    def __init__(self, name):
        self.__name = name

    def get_name(self):
        print("getting name")
        return self.__name

    def set_name(self, value):
        print("setting name")
        self.__name = value

    def delete_name(self):
        print("deleting name")
        del self.__name

    name = property(get_name, set_name, delete_name, "Publisher name")
```

We want to access the name attribute so create a Publisher instance; this example show you the right methods that are being called:

```
>>> p = Publisher("Random House")
>>> p.name
getting name
'Random House'
>>> p.name = "Wolters Kluwer"
setting name
>>> del p.name
deleting name
```

That is all for a basic look at descriptors. If you want a real challenge, look at what you have learned here and attempt to again implement the `@property` decorator – see how you get on.

Chapter 8:
Metaprogramming

Now that you are fully aware that a Python class is an object we can turn to something called metaprogramming. You are already well used to creating functions with the purpose of returning objects so it is unfair to consider these functions as object factories. They take an argument or two, create an object and then they return it. Look at the following example of a function that will create an object called int:

```
In [11]:
def int_factory(s):
    i = int(s)
    return i

i = int_factory('100')
print(i)
100
```

This is a very simple example but every function that you write in any normal program is going to be something along these lines - take your arguments, do a few things (operations) on them and then create your object and return it. However, keeping all of this in mind, there is absolutely nothing to stop you from creating an object that has a type of type (a class, in other words) and then returning it – we call this a metafunction:

```
In [12]:
def class_factory():
    class Foo(object):
```

```
        pass
    return Foo

F = class_factory()
f = F()
print(type(f))
<class '__main__.Foo'>
```

We already know that the `int_factory` function will construct an `int` instance and return it. In the same way, the `class_factory` function will construct an instance of type (a class) and returns it.

However, you may have noticed the slightly awkward construction. If you wanted to do some logic that was perhaps a little more complicated when you construct Foo, you would want, if you could, to avoid the nested indentations and to perhaps give the class a more dynamic definition. We can do this in a fairly easy way – we instantiate Foo directly from type, as in this example:

```
In [13]:
def class_factory():
    return type('Foo', (), {})

F = class_factory()
f = F()
print(type(f))
<class '__main__.Foo'>
```

In fact, the construct
In [14]:

```
class MyClass(object):
    pass
```
is exactly the same as the construct
In [15]:
```
MyClass = type('MyClass', (), {})
```

You should already know by now that `MyClass` is an instance of the type called `type`. We can see that explicitly in version 2 of the definition. There is one confusion that can potentially arise and that is from the way type is more commonly used – as a function that determines an object type. You should work at keeping these two keyword uses separate in your mind; in metafunctions, type is actually a class or a metaclass and `MyClass` is an instance of the type or class.

Let's look at what the type constructor arguments are:

```
type(name, bases, dct)
```

- `name` – this is a string that provides the name of the class that is being constructed
- `bases` – this is a tuple that provides the parent classes of the class under construction
- `dct` – this is a dictionary that provides the methods and the attributes of the class that is being constructed

An example – these two codes will have exactly the same results:

Example 1:

```
In [16]:
class Foo(object):
    i = 4

class Bar(Foo):
    def get_i(self):
        return self.i

b = Bar()
print(b.get_i())
4
```

Example 2:

```
In [17]:
Foo = type('Foo', (), dict(i=4))

Bar = type('Bar', (Foo,), dict(get_i = lambda self: self.i))

b = Bar()
print(b.get_i())
4
```

Although this may seem to you to be a little bit too complicated, it is a very powerful way of creating classes dynamically as you need them,

Custom Metaclasses

Now let's make things a little more interesting. In the same way that you can extend and inherit from a class that you have created; you can also extend and inherit from the type metaclass. You can also create custom behaviors in your metaclass.

Example 1: Attribute Modification

Let's look at a simple example. We are going to create an API and in this API, the user will be able to create a whole set of interfaces which will have a file object in. Every interface must have its own string ID and it must be unique to that interface and each interface will also have its open file object. The user will then have the ability to write specialized methods that will allow them to accomplish specific tasks. There are some good ways of doing this without having to go into metaclasses but this example should hopefully show you clearly what is happening.

First, we are going to create the interface metaclass and it will be derived from type:

```
In [18]:
class InterfaceMeta(type):
    def __new__(cls, name, parents, dct):
        # create a class_id if it has not been specified
        if 'class_id' not in dct:
```

```
        dct['class_id']                =
name.lower()

        # open that specified file so it
can be written to
        if 'file' in dct:
            filename = dct['file']
            dct['file']  =  open(filename,
'w')

        # we must now call type.__new__
to finish off the initialization
        return        super(InterfaceMeta,
cls).__new__(cls, name, parents, dct)
```

Did you spot the modification to the input dictionary (the methods and attributes of your class)? We modified it so that it would add in a class ID if there want one already present and so that the filename would be replaced with a file object that points to the name.

Next, we will use our newly created interface metaclass for the construction and instantiation of a new interface object:

```
In [19]:
Interface   =   InterfaceMeta('Interface',
(), dict(file='tmp.txt'))

print(Interface.class_id)
print(Interface.file)
interface
<open   file   'tmp.txt',   mode   'w'   at
0x21b8810>
```

The behavior of this is exactly as we expect it to be – we have created a `class_id` variable and we have replaced the file class variable with the open file object. However, notice that the interface class creation, using the `InterfaceMeta`, is still a little bit awkward and it isn't that easy to read. This is where `__metaclass__` saves the day. We can do exactly the same thing by defining Interface in a different way:

```
In [20]:
class Interface(object):
    __metaclass__ = InterfaceMeta
    file = 'tmp.txt'

print(Interface.class_id)
print(Interface.file)
interface
<open file 'tmp.txt', mode 'w' at 0x21b8ae0>
```

When we define the `__metaclass__` attribute, we have informed the class that it shouldn't use type to construct the class; we should use `InterfaceMeta` instead. Let's make this a little more definite – note that the Interface type has now been reclassified as `InterfaceMeta`:

```
In [21]:
type(Interface)
Out[21]:
__main__.InterfaceMeta
```

Not only that, any class that is now derived from Interface is going to be constructed from the same metaclass:

```
In [22]:
class UserInterface(Interface):
    file = 'foo.txt'

print(UserInterface.file)
print(UserInterface.class_id)
<open    file    'foo.txt',   mode    'w'    at
0x21b8c00>
userinterface
```

This is a simple way of showing you that metaclasses can be used as way of creating very flexible and incredibly powerful project APIs. An example of that is Django project – this uses these kinds of constructions so that we can use concise declarations of powerful extensions to basic classes.

Example 2: Subclass Registration

There is another way to use metaclasses and that is to register all of the subclasses that are derived from a specific base class automatically. For example, you might have a basic database interface and want the user to have the ability to define interfaces which would then be stored automatically in a master registry. You could go about it this way:

In [23]:
```
class DBInterfaceMeta(type):
    # we will use __init__ instead of __new__ here because we want
    # to be able to modify attributes of this class *after* they have been
    # created
    def __init__(cls, name, bases, dct):
        if not hasattr(cls, 'registry'):
            # this is a base class. Create an empty registry
            cls.registry = {}
        else:
            # this is the derived class. Add cls to the registry
            interface_id = name.lower()
            cls.registry[interface_id] = cls

        super(DBInterfaceMeta, cls).__init__(name, bases, dct)
```

The metaclass is doing a very simple thing here – it is adding a registry dictionary if there isn't already one present. It also adds the newly created class to the registry if that registry is already present. Let's look a bit closer at how this is going to work:

In [24]:
```
class DBInterface(object):
    __metaclass__ = DBInterfaceMeta

print(DBInterface.registry)
{}
```

It's time to create a few subclasses and then make sure that they have been added to the registry:

```
In [25]:
class FirstInterface(DBInterface):
    pass

class SecondInterface(DBInterface):
    pass

class SecondInterfaceModified(SecondInterface):
    pass

print(DBInterface.registry)
{'firstinterface':              <class
'__main__.FirstInterface'>,
'secondinterface':             <class
'__main__.SecondInterface'>,
'secondinterfacemodified':     <class
'__main__.SecondInterfaceModified'>}
```

It works exactly as it should have done. You can use this together with any function that takes implementations from a registry and any of the user-defined objects that are Interface-derived will automatically be accounted for without the user having to register the new types manually.

When Metaclasses Should Be Used

We've looked at a few examples of metaclasses and a few ways in which they can be used in the creation of APIs. Although the metaclass is always working tirelessly away in the background in Python, you rarely have to consider them. The question is though, when do you need to start thinking about using a custom metaclass in a project. This isn't the easiest of questions to answer but this quote may just shed a little light on it for you:

"Metaclasses are deeper magic than 99% of users should ever worry about. If you wonder whether you need them, you don't (the people who actually need them know with certainty that they need them, and don't need an explanation about why)."
– Tim Peters

Chapter 9:
An Overview of Python Scripting Blender

Python is an interactive, interpreted OOP (Object Oriented Programming) language, featuring exceptions, modules, dynamic typing, classes and dynamic, very high-level data types. In short, it combines incredibly clear syntax with incredible power.

Blender is an open-source powerful modeling platform packed full of features that rival any of the professional packages, like Maya and 3D Studio Max. As well as having a full set of modeling tools, Blender is also home to a strong Python API and this allows you to create add-ons and scripts. Best of all, Blender is free.

Python scripts are a very versatile and powerful way of extending the functionality of Blender to the extent that most Blender areas can be scripted, including Import and Export, Animation, Object Creation, Rendering and repetitive task scripting.

Blender works by letting you change the viewport layout to reflect many different ways to work. For example, you might want a set of windows for rendering and then a different set for modeling and the same can be said of scripting Blender features a preset layout for scripting that can be customized as per your requirements.

The Blender interface includes:

- A Text Editor
- A Python Console
- An Info Window
- A Blender Console
- An Interface Elements

Text Editor

This is a standard editor that allows you to edit, load and save your Python script files. You can do all the standard stuff like highlighting syntax and line numbering but there is no option for code completion

Python Console

Combined with the text editor, the Python console provides a very handy way of exploring the Python API in a more efficient way whilst you are coding. The Python console also offers a good Autocomplete feature which lets you explore through the Python API

Info Window

The Info window or viewport in Blender lets you see all the most recent activity in Blender as executable commands. This is a great feature for when you want to prototype a process through the use of modeling methods and then put them into a script.

Blender Console

Blender also features a console window which, in all honesty, is no different to your operating system command prompt. It is useful for printing values when you are testing code.

Bonus Chapter: Django Web Development with Python

Django is a Python web framework that allows for quick development of websites that are secure and easy to maintain. Django was built be very experienced developers to take care of most of the hassle that surrounds web development, leaving you free to write your app without having to go through all the hoops to do it.

Django was first developed between 2003 and 2005 by a team of web developers who started out creating and maintaining a bunch of newspaper websites. Once they had created a few, they started to factor out some of the more common design patterns and code and reuse it. This grew into a generic framework for web development and, in 2005 it was open-sourced as Django.

Over time, Django has grown and it has improved, from its very first release in 2008 right up to the most recent version. Each release has brought bug fixes and new functions, from support for new database types, caching and template engines, right through to generic classes and view functions – this help to cut down on the code that has to be written for several different programming tasks.

As a result, Django is a thriving open-source project, complete with thousands of contributors and users. While there are still some of the original features left, Django has grown into one of the most versatile web development frameworks that ever existed.

With Django, you can write software that is:

Complete

Think of every toy or game that you have ever bought that has the batteries included, so that you can use it straight out of the box. That is Django; it provides just about everything that you might want to do from the off and, because everything is part of the same thing, it all works together seamlessly, follows the same consistent principles of design and it includes the most up to date and extensive documentation.

Versatile

If you can think of a website type, you can almost certainly use Django to build it. It has been used to build Wikis, content management systems, news websites and social networking sites. It works with any client-side framework and it is able to deliver content in just about any format, and that includes RSS feeds, HTML, XML, JSON, etc.

Internally, Django provides you with choices for pretty much any functionality you could want and it can be extended to take in other components as required.

Secure

Django can also help you to avoid many of the more common security errors that are made by providing you with a framework fully engineered to do all the right stuff in giving your website automatic protection. For example, it can give you a highly secure way of managing user accounts, managing passwords, avoiding simple but common errors like using cookies to store session information – this makes that information highly vulnerable; a cookie merely stores a key while the data should be stored in a database. It also helps you avoid storing passwords instead of the password hash.

For those that don't know, a password hash is a value of fixed length that is created when a password is sent through a cryptographic hash function. Django is able to see if the password that has been entered is the right one by putting it through the hash function and checking the output against the hash value in storage.

Django also provides protection by default against a wide range of known vulnerabilities, such as cross-site scripting, SQL injection, clickjacking and cross-site request forgery.

Scalable

The component-based architecture that Django uses dictates that each bit of the architecture is completely independent of all the other bits; that means they can be changed or replaced as needed. By having this type of separation, increased traffic can be scaled for through the addition of hardware at any level, such as database servers, caching servers and application servers.

Maintainable

Design patterns and principles that encourage reusable and maintainable code is what is used in Django. It makes good use of the DRY principle – Don't Repeat Yourself – meaning there is no duplication that is not necessary and this, in turn, cuts the amount of code needed. Django promotes grouping of functionality that is related into applications that are reusable and also groups code that is related into modules.

Portable

Django is based in Python and this makes it possible that it runs on several different platforms. This means that you are not stuck with using just one specified platform and your applications will run on all the different implementations of Mac, Windows, and Linux. As well as that, Django is thoroughly supported by several different web hosting providers and these will provide you with the right infrastructure and the right documentation for hosting a Django website.

What Django Code Looks Like

In a traditional website, one that is data-driven, the web applications will wait for the HTTP requests to come from the client, such as a web browser. When that request has been received, the application will use the URL and some information from both GET and POST data to work out what is needed. Depending on the requirements, information may then be read or written from a database or another task may be performed. The application then returns the response to the browser and it will often insert the data it has retrieved into a placeholder within an HTML template to create an HTML page.

In a Django web application, the code that is responsible for handling each of the following steps into their own files:

- **URL** – while requests from each and every URL can be processed through one function, it is better and easier to maintain if a separate view function is written to for each resource. In order for the HTTP requests to be directed to the right view, based on the URL, a URL mapper is used. This is also able to match digit or string patterns that show up in a URL and pass them as data to a view function.

- **View** – this is a request handler function and it will receive an HTTP request and return it as an HTTP response. The views will access the data that is needed to satisfy a request through models and it will delegate response formatting to templates

- **Model** – a model is a Python object that is used to define the structure of the data in an application It also provides the mechanisms needed to add, modify and delete as well as querying database records.
- **Template** – this is a text file that is used to define the layout or the structure of a file, like an HTML page, using placeholders as a representation of the content. Views will create HTML pages

dynamically through the use of an HTML template and will populate it with data that comes from a model. The template is a method of defining structure in any file type, not just HTML

Conclusion

Thank you again for owning this book!

I hope this book was able to help you to improve and further your knowledge on Python computer programming.

The next step is to practice, that's all. Computer programming concepts change regularly; old ones disappear or are updated and new ones appear and, if you don't keep up with it, you will lose it. You have come so far; the last thing you want to do is have to start again.

There are plenty of resources for you to choose from on the internet; books, forums, and courses, all of which will help you go further in your quest to become a top Python programmer.

Finally, if you enjoyed this book, then I'd like to ask you for a favor, would you be kind enough to leave a review for this book on Amazon? It'd be greatly appreciated!

Thank you and good luck!

A Preview Of 'Python: Tips and Tricks to Programming Code with Python'

"Image Colors"

Let's start this with some fun image programming. It's always nice to have some fun programming up your sleeve, and this code will give you just that.

In this chapter we will look at codes to help you change the color of an image, so you can make it look the way you want it to. This code will give you some fun things to do to your images when coding. It's also just a fun thing to play around with.

1. Type the following in a Python IDLE window.

```
CODE:

from ImageLibrary import *
myfile=pickAFile()
pict=makePicture(myfile)
show(pic)
```

This tells Python to use every function that is in your image library.

This should not be done in a main window. You need to write this in a new window. Do this by choosing, "file -> New Window" and then paste the code in an empty window, then pick "run". You will then be asked if want to save your file. The file needs to be saved in an arbitrary location.

The "`from ImageLibrary import*`" needs to be placed into every IDLE window. `myfile=pickAFile()` lets the computer know you need a window that you can pick the .jpg image file that you want to play with.

The picture should be small so that everything doesn't take a long time. `pickAFile()` will give you a return of the full name of your image file.

2. Ask Python to print myfile so you will be able to see how the image looks. As a reminder, print command looks like print myfile.

The string should look like:
`C:/Users/Public/Pictures/image.jpg`

That means `myfile` is a string that states the picture that you want. You could use a string so you won't have to call `pickAFile()` each time that you need anything new.

Like this:
`pic=makePicture("/users/nameGoesHere/Pictures/image.jpg")`

Make your picture:
```
from ImageLibrary import *
filename=pickAFile()
pic=makePicture(filename)
show(pic)
```

This will load you picture into memory so you can change it. You don't need to call `makePicture(myfile)` unless you plan on putting the results in a useful place such as assigning it to a variable such as `pic`.

Make sure that you get the lower and upper case letters right because Python is case sensitive.

Whenever you change something about the picture, you have to call `show(pic)` so you will be able to see your changes. Your changes do not update automatically when they are changed.

3. Open the image and display it

CODE:

```
from ImageLibrary import *
myfile=pickAFile()
pic=makePicture(myfile)
show(pic)
```

First thing you are going to do is make every red pixel level to 255:

```
for p in getPixels(pict):
     setRed(p,255)
show(pic)
```

3a. Change red, green, and blue levels until the image is black, then white, the green.

Another neat function is `setColor(pixel,color)` will change a pixel color. The list of predefined colors are cyan, magenta, pink, orange, yellow, darkGrey, lightGrey, grey, blue, green, red, black, white. You can also use this function to change a pixel color to orange instead of the regular blue, red, and green colors.

3b. Change the picture color using the for loop, setColor (pixel, color), and then you can use the colors that have already been defined.

You can also use `makeColor(redValue, greenValue, blueValue)`. This lets you create any color you want. To make purple you use:
`Purple=makeColor (255, 0, 255)`

3c. Play with r, g, b values to figure out how to create yellow color. Use the earlier code to make the change to the complete picture.

You can use the makeLighter (color) function to lighten parts of color. It actually subtracts 40 from each main color green, red, and blue. This also can be used to lighten the whole photo.

```
for p in getPixels(pic):
    col=getColor(p)
    makeLighter(col)
    setColor(p, col)
```

You can also use `makeDarker(color)` that will make the picture darker.

3d. Apply the `makeDarker` to each pixel three times.

What will happen?

You may possibly see an error such as:

`CODE:`

```
Traceback (most recent call last):
    File
"/User/name/Documents/jmss/exercise1.py",
line 14 <module>
        show(file)
    File
"/User/name/Documents/ImageLibrary.py",
line 230, in show
        resolution = (picture.getWidth(),
picture.getHeight ())
AttributeError: 'str' object has no
attribute 'getWidth'
```

If this is the case, don't panic. Look at the line number and filename. They refer back to the file. This is talking about `show(file)`. With this error you can see show was being called with file - and not that of a picture.

Many of your errors will probably look like this; innocent mistakes that you can easily fix.

Now you know this neat tip on how to change the coloring of an image just in case you want to. This is a great tool to have when you want to add some fun images to your website or app.

To learn more about this book, search the title: "Python: Tips and Tricks" (by: Charlie Masterson) on the search box found in the Amazon.com website.

About the Author

Charlie Masterson is a computer programmer and instructor who have developed several applications and computer programs.

As a computer science student, he got interested in programming early but got frustrated learning the highly complex subject matter.

Charlie wanted a teaching method that he could easily learn from and develop his programming skills. He soon discovered a teaching series that made him learn faster and better.

Applying the same approach, Charlie successfully learned different programming languages and is now teaching the subject matter through writing books.
With the books that he writes on computer programming, he hopes to provide great value and help readers interested to learn computer-related topics.

Made in the USA
Lexington, KY
04 June 2017